CW00322213

LEICESTER
TIGERS
Official Yearbook 2003-04

Copyright 2003 Leicester Tigers Rugby Club.
All rights reserved. No part of this publication may be
reproduced, stored in a retrieval system, or transmitted, in any
form or by any means without the prior written permission of
the publisher, nor be otherwise circulated in any binding or
cover other than that in which it is published and without a
similar condition being imposed on the subsequent purchaser.
Acknowledgements: The publishers would like to thank Stuart
Farmer Media Services and OPTA for supplying statistics.

SIDANPRESS
Passionate about rugby
Copyright © Sidan Press Ltd 2003.

Club Directory

LEICESTER
TIGERS

Ground:
Welford Road Stadium,
Aylestone Road,
Leicester LE2 7TR
Phone: 08701 28 34 30
Fax: 0116 285 4766
E-mail: tigers@tigers.co.uk

Chairman: Peter Tom

Chief Executive: Peter Wheeler

Managing Director: David Clayton

Company Secretary: Mary Ford

Directors:
David Abell, Garry Adey, John Allen,
Bob Beason, Roy Jackson,
David Jones, David Matthews

President: Bob Rowell

Director of Rugby: Dean Richards

Coaches: John Wells, Andy Key, Damien McGrath

Life Members:
John Allen, Jerry Day, Chalkie White

Press & PR
Sam Rossiter-Stead
Phone: 0116 2171 284
Fax: 0116 2171 291
E-mail: srs@tigers.co.uk

Corporate Sales
Mike Stevens
E-mail: sales@tigers.co.uk
Phone: 0116 2171 293
Fax: 0116 2171 292

Ticket Office
Jean Parr
Phone: 08701 28 34 30
Fax: 0116 2171 263
E-mail: tickets@tigers.co.uk

Conference and Banqueting
Mandy North
Phone: 0116 2171 278
E-mail: cab@tigers.co.uk

Community
Jim Overend
Phone: 0116 2171 253
E-mail: jim.overend@tigers.co.uk

Merchandise
Sara Watson
Phone: 0116 2171 267
E-mail: shop@tigers.co.uk

Supporter Services
Paul Hayes
Phone: 0116 2171 226
E-mail: paul.hayes@tigers.co.uk

Stadium Management
Clive Mountford
Phone: 0116 2171 255
E-mail: clive.mountford@tigers.co.uk

Academy, Youth & U21
Andy Key
E-mail: andy.key@tigers.co.uk

Contents

5	Welcome
6	Honours and Records
7	Milestones
10	August & September Reports
20	September Review
22	October Reports
30	October Review
32	November Reports
42	November Review
44	December Reports
52	December Review
54	January Reports
62	January Review
64	February Report
68	February Review
70	March Reports
74	March Review
76	April Reports
84	April Review
86	May Reports
96	May Review
98	2002-03 Season Stats
100	Tigers Extras Review
102	Leicester XV v Barbarians
104	Tigers Squad 2002/03 Photo
106	Senior Coaches
110	Player Profiles
130	Tigers U21s Squad Photo
132	U21 Season Review
134	U21 Picture Special
136	Tigers Youth
139	Academy Coaches
142	Academy Profiles
152	Stadium Bar Guide
154	Tickets
156	Community
158	Members
160	Adams Junior Tiger Club
162	Conference & Banqueting
164	Website
166	Opposition – Bath Rugby
168	Opposition – Gloucester
170	Opposition – Leeds Tykes
172	Opposition – London Irish
174	Opposition – London Wasps
176	Opposition – NEC Harlequins
178	Opposition – Newcastle Falcons
180	Opposition – Northampton Saints
182	Opposition – Rotherham
184	Opposition – Saracens
186	Opposition – Sharks
188	Pre-season
189	European Preview
190	Season Preview
191	Tigers Fixtures 2003-04

winning comes naturally

Part of Aggregate Industries plc and the new official main sponsor of Leicester Tigers, Bradstone have won a string of awards for innovative garden landscaping products, outstanding customer service and eye-catching brochures. It's a real winning combination!

(f) **01335 372222**

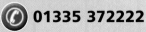

OFFICIALMAINSPONSOR

An AGGREGATE INDUSTRIES PLC business

Welcome

This is the first edition of the Leicester Tigers Yearbook and I hope it will be the first of many in the years ahead.

The yearbook contains a wealth of information about Tigers, including match by match reports and analysis, statistics, player biographies, and a very useful away grounds section.

The yearbook will not only provide an immediate source of reference, it will also through words and pictures enable you to relive memories of games gone by and the highs and lows a season brings.

Year by year the yearbook will develop into the history of Leicester Tigers, and I'm sure will occupy pride of place on the bookshelves of Tigers fans around the world.

I would also like to thank our supporters and sponsors for making Tigers the club it is today. The last 123 years have seen many changes to the club, but the one thing that has remained constant is the incredible levels of support and the family atmosphere.

The game itself has also changed significantly and it is now faster and more physical than ever before. We have adapted very well to the modern era and I'm confident there's a great future ahead for Leicester Tigers.

Thank you once again for all your continued support.

I hope you enjoy the book.

Peter Tom
Chairman

Honours & Records

Roll of Honour

European Champions
2001-02, 2000-01

English Champions
2001-02, 2000-01, 1999-2000,
1998-99, 1994-95, 1987-88

English Cup Winners
1996-1997, 1992-1993,
1980-1981, 1979-1980,
1978-1979

Championship Winners
2000-01

Most Appearances

Name	Career	Games
David Matthews	1955-1974	502
Sid Penny	1896-1910	491
John Allen	1961-1975	457
Doug Norman	1920-1933	453
Paul Dodge	1975-1993	434+3
Dusty Hare	1976-1989	393+1
Pedlar Wood	1906-1922	388
Garry Adey	1967-1981	381
John Wells	1982-1997	360+7
Steve Kenney	1975-1990	361+4
Les Cusworth	1978-1990	365
George Ward	1910-1926	361
Jacky Braithwaite	1895-1906	359
Billy Foreman	1893-1906	358
Bob Rowell	1962-1978	355

Most Tries

Name	Career	Games	Tries
Percy Lawrie	1907-1924	318	206
Barry Evans	1981-1995	272+1	170
John Duggan	1970-1980	302	158
Bob Barker	1968-1979	318+2	158
Harry Wilkinson	1895-1905	233	153
Teddy Haselmere	1918-1923	180	136
Rory Underwood	1983-1997	230+6	134
David Matthews	1955-1974	502	119
Ralph Buckingham	1924-1935	325	117
Harold Day	1919-1929	212	108
Neil Back	1990-2003	274+16	108
Dean Richards	1982-1997	306+8	105
Pedlar Wood	1906-1922	388	102

Most Points

Name	Career	Games	T	C	PG	DG	GM	Pts
Dusty Hare	1976-1989	393+1	87	779	820	47	-	4507
John Liley	1988-1997	226+4	74	417	449	2	-	2518
Tim Stimpson	1998-2003	136+9	30	216	355	2	-	1653
Jez Harris	1984-1996	213+12	23	165	178	70	-	1171
Harold Day	1919-1929	212	108	281	81	4	2	1151
Bob Barker	1968-1979	318+2	158	92	107	2	-	1117

Key: **T** - Tries **Con** - Conversions **PG** - Penalty Goal **DG** - Drop Goal **GM** - Goal from a mark **Pts** - Points

Milestones 1880-1930

1880

Aug 3 - Leicester Football Club formed in a meeting at the George Hotel in Leicester from an amalgamation of three clubs: Leicester Societies AFC, Leicester Amateur FC and Leicester Alert.

Oct 23 - First match against Moseley, played at the Belgrave Cricket and Cycle Ground ends in a nil-all draw. Original club colours were black and Leicester were known as "The Death or Glory Boys".

Jan 8 - First game at Victoria Park, new home venue.

1882

Oct 7 - Return to the Belgrave Cricket and Cycle Ground for one season only

1885

Feb 21 - The earliest reference to the now famous Tiger nickname appears in the Leicester Daily Post stating "the Tiger stripes were keeping well together."

1888

Sep 29 - Club move back to the Belgrave Cricket & Cycle Ground from Victoria Park

1889

Apr 4 - Leicester reach their first ever final, but lose to Coventry 0-8 at Rugby in the Midland Counties Cup.

1891

Leicester wear their famous scarlet, green and white colours for the first time although in a vertical stripe formation.

1892

Sep 16 - The current home ground Welford Road opens with a game against the Leicestershire Rugby Union, won 17-0.

1895

Sep 25 - Club switch to scarlet, green and white hoops for the first time

1898

Apr 6 - The Tigers win their first ever trophy by beating Moseley 5-3 in the final of the Midland Counties Cup at Coventry. They go on to win this competition for the next seven seasons until retiring "to give other teams a chance".

1902

Feb 8 - Welford Road's first international match sees England beat Ireland 6-3.

1903

Jack Miles becomes the club's first international player

1909

Sep 4 - New Clubhouse opened for game vs Stratford-upon-Avon containing for the first time dressing rooms at the ground

29 Dec - First fixture against the Barbarians ends in a 9-all draw.

1912

Mar 9 - Harry Lawrie becomes the first Tiger to be sent off in a game at Harlequins by referee HA Taylor.

1918

Dec 26 - New Members' Stand officially opened for the first Tigers game in 3 1/2 years for the game against the 4th Leicestershire Regiment. On the same day Percy Lawrie with his 154th try overtakes Harry Wilkinson as the club's leading try scorer, he eventually finishes with a still unsurpassed 206 tries.

1920

Oct 2 - New stand (later named the Crumbie Stand) opened by President of the Rugby Union, Ernest Prescott.

1922

Dec 30 - Alastair Smallwood sets a club record by scoring seven tries in the same game in the 36-0 hammering of Manchester at Welford Road.

1923

Feb 10 - England beat Ireland 23-5 at Welford Road in the last England home international played away from Twickenham until 1992.

1926

Sep 4 - The Leicester forwards first regularly wear letters as a means of identification against Bath at Welford Road.

1927

Mar 26 - Harold Day becomes the first Tiger to score 1,000 career points at home to Old Merchant Tailors.

1928

Mar 13 - Tom Crumbie, Hon sec from 1895 dies in office.

1930

Nov 29 - The first BBC radio broadcast of a Tigers game sees Leicester beat Waterloo 21-5 at Welford Road.

Milestones 1931-1990

1931

Sep 5 - Against Bath at Welford Road marks the first occasion that an entire Leicester team is lettered.

1946

Dec 14 - Leicester's first replacement is Haydn Thomas who takes over from JCK Campbell at Blackheath when the former is late in arriving.

1951

Feb 3 - First TV appearance against London Scottish on the Richmond Athletic Ground, won 14-0.

1956

Nov 18 - Tigers first game on a Sunday sees them lose to Old Belvedere in Dublin 3-23.

1959

Oct 22 - Clocks unveiled on stands as a tribute to the late Eric Thorneloe who was Honorary Secretary between 1928-57.

1960

Feb 13 - Tigers' first game under lights was at Newport, which they lost 9-19.

1963

Dec 14 - David Matthews misses the visit of Blackheath to Welford Road and thus breaks his run of 109 successive first team appearances stretching back to January 1961.

1964

Oct 8 - Floodlights first used at Welford Road for a game against a Midlands XV, won 31-8.

1971

Nov 21 - Leicester's first 'modern' cup tie sees them lose 3-10 to Nottingham at Beeston on a Sunday in the first round of the RFU Knockout Cup.

1973

Apr 21 - David Matthews breaks Sid Penny's club appearance record with his 492nd First XV game at Broughton Park. He goes onto to make 502 appearances.

1977

Sep 6 - New scoreboard unveiled

1978

Apr 15 - The club reach their first Twickenham final but are beaten 3-6 by Gloucester.

Dec 27 - Clubhouse extension opened.

1979

Apr 21 - Leicester win the John Player Cup for the first time, beating Moseley 15-12 in the final at Twickenham.

1980

Apr 19 - Dusty Hare breaks Harold Day's record Tigers career points aggregate with his 1,152nd point, kicked on the day that Leicester retained the John Player Cup with a 21-9 victory over London Irish at Twickenham.

Aug 6 - To honour the centenary of the club's foundation, Leicester become the first English club side to embark on a tour to the Southern Hemisphere. They play six games in Australia and Fiji, only losing the opening game to Queensland.

1981

May 2 - Tigers win the John Player Cup for a 3rd successive season when they beat Gosforth 22-15 in the final, and are allowed to keep the original trophy which is now on display at the Clubhouse.

1984

Feb 18 - A club record seven players appear in England team against Ireland at Twickenham

1985

Sep 14 - New changing room, medical and weights rooms opened under the Crumbie Stand.

1986

Sep 17 - Dusty Hare scores a club record 43 points in a game in the 95-6 trouncing of Birmingham at Welford Road.

1988

Apr 4 - Leicester are confirmed as the inaugural Courage League champions with a 39-15 victory over Waterloo at Welford Road.

1989

Jan 28 - Les Cusworth drops a club record 4 goals at Liverpool St Helens in the 3rd round of the cup.

1990

(Summer) - Tony Russ is appointed the club's first full-time coach

Milestones 1991-2003

1991

Oct 13 - New Zealand beat Italy 31-21 in the qualifying stages of the World Cup at Welford Road.

1992

Apr 11 - Tigers achieve their record points total in a game by demolishing Liverpool St Helens 100-0 at Welford Road.

Sep 5 - Welford Road celebrates its centenary with two special matches. The first sees Leicester lose out 11-18 to an England XV and then overcome a Leicestershire XV 40-20 four days later.

1993

May 1 - Leicester win the Pilkington Cup by beating Harlequins 23-16 in the final at Twickenham.

Sep 18 - The new 18 foot electronic scoreboard is unveiled for the match against Orrell.

1995

Apr 29 - Tigers win the Courage League for a second time after beating Bristol 17-3 in front of 13,000 at Welford Road.

Sep 23 - The new 3,000 seat Alliance & Leicester stand is used for the first time for the visit of Bath, and officially opened with a game against Transvaal on 20 November.

1996

Jan - Peter Wheeler is appointed the club's first Chief Executive.

May 30 - Bob Dwyer is appointed Director of Rugby.

1997

Jan 25 - Tigers reach the final of the Heineken European Cup after English teams enter the competition for the first time. In the final at Cardiff Arms Park they are overwhelmed 28-9, by a superb team performance from French side Brive.

Apr 2 - A record six Leicester players are named in the British Lions squad to tour South Africa, including the captain Martin Johnson. Later the same day, Tigers beat Wasps 18-12 in front of a record English league crowd of 17,000 at Welford Road.

May 10 - Leicester win the Pilkington Cup by beating Sale 9-3 in the final at Twickenham.

Dec 8 - Tigers become a plc after a successful share issue raises vital funds.

1998

Feb 17 - Dean Richards takes over as Director of Rugby.

1999

May 2 - Tigers clinch a third league title when they take the Allied Dunbar Premiership with a 21-12 victory over Newcastle Falcons at Kingston Park.

Oct 10 - Welford Road hosts a Rugby World Cup game for the second time as Tonga shock Italy 28-25.

2000

May 14 - Leicester claim a second successive Premiership crown following a 30-23 win at Bristol's Memorial Stadium.

2001

Mar 17 - Take a third Premiership crown in a row when Bath beat Wasps at the Rec, an hour or so after the Tigers had demolished the Falcons 51-7 at Welford Road.

May 13 - Leicester claim the inaugural Zurich Championship crown when they beat Bath 22-10 in the final at Twickenham.

May 19 - Tigers win the European Heineken Cup for the first time, beating Paris based Stade Français in the final at Parc des Princes 34-30.

Summer - Martin Johnson becomes the first player ever to captain the British Lions on two separate tours, when he leads them in Australia.

2002

Apr 13 - A fourth consecutive Premiership is wrapped up with a 20-10 victory over Newcastle at Welford Road.

May 25 - Leicester become the first club to retain the European Heineken Cup by beating Irish Province Munster 15-9 in the final at Cardiff's Millennium Stadium.

2003

May 31 - Tigers qualify for the 2003/04 European Heineken Cup with a thrilling extra time victory over Saracens at Franklin's Gardens, Northampton to pick up the Zurich Wildcard.

Leeds Tykes
26

Tries: Scarbrough (2) **Cons:** Van Straaten, Ross
Pens: Ross (3) **DGs:** Ross

Position	No.	Player
Full Back	15	D.Scarbrough
Right Wing	14	G.Harder
Centre	13	T.Davies
Centre	12	B.Van Straaten
Left Wing	11	D.Albanese
Fly Half	10	G.Ross
Scrum Half	9	D.Hegarty
Prop	1	J.Wring
Hooker	2	M.Regan
Prop	3	M.Shelley (c)
Lock	4	C.Murphy
Lock	5	T.Palmer
Flanker	6	C.Mather
Flanker	7	D.Hyde
No.8	8	I.Feau'nati

Replacements: S.Campbell, A.Dickens, C.Emmerson, C.Hall, C.Hogg, M.Holt, G.Kerr

Leicester Tigers lost out to last season's bottom-placed side, Leeds Tykes, in a disappointing start to the season at Headingley.

Leeds opened up the scoring with a try after 14 minutes courtesy of full back Dan Scarbrough. Fly half Braam Van Straaten converted and Leeds added a penalty before the break to leave the half-time score at 10-3 to the Yorkshiremen.

Stimpson's solitary penalty came after a period of intense pressure from Leicester, but a solid Tykes defence kept the European Champions away from the line with the visitors picking up just three points in the half.

> "The players are sat in the dressing room looking like they've lost the European Cup final." – **Dean Richards**

Tigers drew level after the break with some clever thinking from fly half Austin Healey. The attack was generated by centre Ollie Smith with support from Steve Booth who danced further into the Tykes half.

Healey took on the challenge and passed out to Neil Back who fixed two defenders before passing back to Healey who crossed in the corner. Stimpson converted to put Tigers in contention for the win.

Despite adding a second penalty to their tally, Tigers were unable to seal the victory and two more penalties from makeshift Tykes boot Gordon

Did you know?
This game saw Tigers wearing a shirt primarily white in colour for the first time since they played Waterloo in 1960.

13 Leicester Tigers

Tries: Healey **Cons:** Stimpson
Pens: Stimpson (2)

Ross, and an injury time try from Scarbrough put the nail in the coffin and Tigers in the bottom half of the table with a 26-13 loss.

Position	No.	Player
Full Back	15	T.Stimpson
Right Wing	14	S.Booth
Centre	13	O.Smith
Centre	12	D.Hipkiss
Left Wing	11	F.Tuilagi
Fly Half	10	A.Healey
Scrum Half	9	J.Hamilton
Prop	1	G.Rowntree
Hooker	2	D.West
Prop	3	F.Tournaire
Lock	4	M.Johnson (c)
Lock	5	B.Kay
Flanker	6	J.Kronfeld
Flanker	7	N.Back
No.8	8	M.Corry

Replacements: G.Chuter, J.Naufahu, H.Ellis, P.Freshwater, W.Johnson, S.Vesty, P.Short

Match Stats		
Tackles	184	116
Missed Tackles	23	25
Ball Carries	91	118
Metres	478	721
Defenders Beaten	23	19
Passes	125	162
Clean Breaks	2	0
Pens / Free Kicks	15	13
Turnovers	12	23
Breakdowns Won	82	81
% Line-Outs Won	85	100
% Scrums Won	100	95

Leicester Tigers 30

Tries: Back, Booth, Hamilton, Stimpson
Cons: Stimpson (2) **Pens:** Stimpson (2)

Position	No.	Player
Full Back	15	T.Stimpson
Right Wing	14	S.Booth
Centre	13	O.Smith
Centre	12	J.Naufahu
Left Wing	11	F.Tuilagi
Fly Half	10	A.Healey
Scrum Half	9	H.Ellis
Prop	1	G.Rowntree
Hooker	2	D.West
Prop	3	F.Tournaire
Lock	4	M.Johnson (c)
Lock	5	B.Kay
Flanker	6	M.Corry
Flanker	7	N.Back
No.8	8	W.Johnson

Replacements: G.Chuter, P.Freshwater, J.Hamilton, D.Hipkiss, J.Kronfeld, P.Short, S.Vesty

Tigers clocked up a comfortable win over Harlequins at Welford Road, beating the visitors 30-6 in their first home Premiership match of the season. In a game that didn't come to life until the final quarter, Tigers outscored Harlequins by four tries to none.

A Tim Stimpson penalty put the Tigers into the lead after just three minutes of play but the visitors were quick to even the score with an almost identical David Slemen penalty kick. Following a Harlequins lineout deep in the Tigers' half, an impressive break by new centre Jo Naufahu took play back into Harlequins territory and sloppy play by the visitors gave away a penalty which was an easy opportunity for Tim Stimpson to put more points on the board. The match continued with Tigers trying to punch holes in the Harlequins defence all to no avail.

Poor Harlequins discipline eventually gave Tigers the chance to capitalise on a series of penalties kicked to touch. The forwards' persistence paid off with a drive over the line and a trademark Neil Back try converted by Tim Stimpson in the 24th minute.

> "Following last week's game everyone took a long, hard look at themselves. Players have responded to make a reasonable performance today."
> **– Dean Richards**

Play continued with Harlequins hungry to score, but despite two penalties conceded by Tigers in front of the posts, both Slemen kicks went wide leaving the half-time score at 13-6.

A slow start to the second half was epitomised by messy and broken play from both sides. Nearly 20 minutes after the restart, a well-timed miss-pass in the Tigers' backs and penetrating runs by both Healey and Hamilton led to an excellent catch and give by Josh Kronfeld which created an overlap for Steve Booth who scampered over the line on the right.

The game suddenly sparked to life in the final quarter with a rally of kicks which eventually gave Tigers the opportunity to score with a scrum ten metres off the try line. Despite Kronfeld's driving run

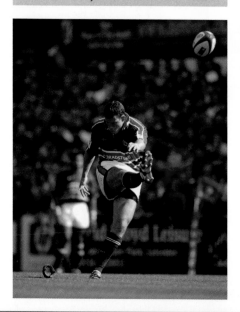

6 NEC Harlequins

Pens: Slemen [2]

and dive over the line, the big man was held up by a determined Quins defence. A second scrum was given and scrum half Hamilton put the ball over the line following a strong drive by the forwards. A better-placed kick by Stimpson saw the try converted.

The game continued to gather momentum on both sides but Quins were unable to make the most of their possession and penalties. Strong work in the lineouts led to Tigers stealing a lot of Quins ball. A penalty in the Harlequins' half well into injury time gave Tigers the chance to further their lead when fly half Austin Healy opted to kick to touch. A great take in the lineout by Peter Short drew in the Quins defence and gave the backs space to work their magic. In the last play of the game, Booth set up a try for Stimpson who dived over the line in the right hand corner. Stimpson failed to convert his own try, missing out on the opportunity to become the first Premiership player to score 1,000 points, but with a bonus point for the four Tigers tries and a convincing 30-6 win, the inspirational full back had plenty to be happy about.

Position	No.	Player
Full Back	15	N.Williams
Right Wing	14	M.Moore
Centre	13	W.Greenwood
Centre	12	C.Bell
Left Wing	11	B.Gollings
Fly Half	10	D.Sleman
Scrum Half	9	M.Powell
Prop	1	J.Leonard [c]
Hooker	2	A.Tiatia
Prop	3	L.Gomez
Lock	4	K.Rudzki
Lock	5	B.Davison
Flanker	6	L.Sherriff
Flanker	7	P.Sanderson
No.8	8	T.Diprose

Replacements: S.Bemand, M.Caputo, J.Evans, R.Jewell, S.Miall, V.Satala, B.Starr

Match Stats	TIGERS	NEC
Tackles	84	83
Missed Tackles	9	13
Ball Carries	78	77
Metres	426	409
Defenders Beaten	10	9
Passes	138	115
Clean Breaks	7	0
Pens / Free Kicks	11	11
Turnovers	20	17
Breakdowns Won	66	68
% Line-Outs Won	88	74
% Scrums Won	100	93

Sharks 29

Tries: Walshe, Jones **Cons:** Hodgson (2)
Pens: Hodgson (5)

Position	No.	Player
Full Back	15	J.Robinson
Right Wing	14	M.Cueto
Centre	13	J.Baxendell
Centre	12	D.Harris
Left Wing	11	S.Hanley
Fly Half	10	C.Hodgson
Scrum Half	9	B.Redpath (c)
Prop	1	J.Thorp
Hooker	2	A.Titterrell
Prop	3	B.Stewart
Lock	4	C.Jones
Lock	5	S.Lines
Flanker	6	A.Sanderson
Flanker	7	S.Pinkerton
No.8	8	P.Anglesea

Replacements: M.Deane, D.Schofield, V.Going, C.Marais, A.Perelini, N.Walshe, K.Yates

Tigers suffered their second away defeat of the season at Heywood Road, going down 29-16 to a committed Sale outfit in front of a full house.

The visitors started brightly enough with a Tim Stimpson penalty on seven minutes giving them a 3-0 lead and taking the full back past 1,000 Premiership points.

That was the end of the good news, however, as Charlie Hodgson kicked three penalties of his own on 10, 18 and 25 minutes to take his side into a 9-3 lead.

Although Tigers had plenty of possession and territory they could not create a scoring opportunity and it was Sharks who could have scored had Dan Harris and England full back Jason Robinson received better passes from their teammates.

> "We put a lot of pressure on Sale but we let them back in and it comes back to decision making." – Dean Richards

Stimpson and Hodgson both found the mark again before half-time and Sale increased their advantage three minutes into the second period.

Harris made a good run but was stopped just short and set up a ruck allowing replacement scrum half Nick Walshe to dive over the line for a fine score. Hodgson converted for a 19-6 lead.

Sale's Andy Titterrell and Tigers' Martin Corry received yellow cards after 50 minutes and visiting Director of Rugby Dean Richards responded by throwing on England forwards Graham Rowntree, Dorian West and Neil Back.

Leicester sprung into life and managed to put together the best passage of play of the match with phase after phase of superb ball retention.

Eventually the home line cracked and number nine Harry

16 Leicester Tigers

Tries: Ellis **Cons:** Stimpson
Pens: Stimpson (3)

Ellis darted over on the blind side for a try which Stimpson converted.

It was all Tigers at this stage and more sustained pressure gave Stimpson the opportunity for a sharp snap at goal to reduce the deficit to a mere three points.

The comeback was thwarted, however, when a stray Healey chip found Sale second row Chris Jones who caught the ball inside his own half and sprinted fully 50 metres to score under the posts, despite a last-ditch tackle from Healey.

Hodgson converted and added a penalty on 76 minutes to complete the scoring.

Tigers continued to hammer away at the home line but there was no way through and they travelled home empty handed for the second time in a fortnight.

Position	No.	Player
Full Back	15	T.Stimpson
Right Wing	14	S.Booth
Centre	13	G.Gelderbloom
Centre	12	J.Naufahu
Left Wing	11	F.Tuilagi
Fly Half	10	A.Healey
Scrum Half	9	H.Ellis
Prop	1	P.Freshwater
Hooker	2	G.Chuter
Prop	3	F.Tournaire
Lock	4	M.Johnson (c)
Lock	5	L.Deacon
Flanker	6	P.Short
Flanker	7	J.Kronfeld
No.8	8	M.Corry

Replacements: G.Rowntree, D.West, D.Hipkiss, B.Kay, S.Vesty, T.Tierney, N.Back

Did you know?
This match saw Austin Healey score his fourth drop goal for the club - the previous ones were against Leinster in 1997, Gloucester and Pontypridd in 2000.

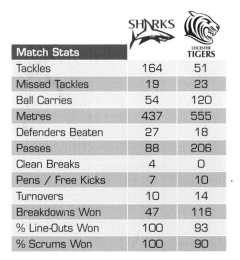

Match Stats	SHARKS	TIGERS
Tackles	164	51
Missed Tackles	19	23
Ball Carries	54	120
Metres	437	555
Defenders Beaten	27	18
Passes	88	206
Clean Breaks	4	0
Pens / Free Kicks	7	10
Turnovers	10	14
Breakdowns Won	47	116
% Line-Outs Won	100	93
% Scrums Won	100	90

Leicester Tigers 52

Tries: Kafer, Back, Smith, Rowntree **Cons:** Stimpson (4)
Pens: Stimpson (7) **DGs:** Stimpson

Position	No.	Player
Full Back	15	T.Stimpson
Right Wing	14	H.Ellis
Centre	13	O.Smith
Centre	12	R.Kafer
Left Wing	11	F.Tuilagi
Fly Half	10	S.Vesty
Scrum Half	9	T.Tierney
Prop	1	G.Rowntree
Hooker	2	D.West
Prop	3	D.Garforth
Lock	4	M.Johnson (c)
Lock	5	B.Kay
Flanker	6	L.Moody
Flanker	7	N.Back
No.8	8	M.Corry

Replacements: S.Booth, G.Gelderbloom, J.Naufahu, G.Chuter, J.Kronfeld, P.Short, F.Tournaire

Leicester Tigers found their form at a packed Welford Road, beating Newcastle Falcons 52-9. In a match in which Leicester were the dominant force, on-form full back Tim Stimpson added to his already impressive kicking record by equalling the Premiership record for points scored in one match with 32 points.

The game kicked off well with Tigers securing a score on the board after the first four minutes with a Stimpson penalty. However, both teams were over-eager to dominate play early on which led to a series of mistakes and penalties conceded in the first quarter of the game.

> "It was a great debut. I'm just glad it's out of the way. Today we kept our composure. Stimpson's kicking helped so we could relax a bit more and play a bit freer."
> – Sam Vesty

Tigers' early score was soon levelled by England fly-half Jonny Wilkinson who made it 6-6 in the first ten minutes. But Falcons' poor discipline was converted into points by Stimpson, who kicked six penalties and a fantastic drop goal in the first half.

Despite early threats by Newcastle, including a break by centre Jamie Noon, the awesome Tigers' defence kept the visitors at bay and towards the end of the first half persistent play in the Tigers' back line gave Rod Kafer an overlap to score left of the posts in his first game of the season.

A try-saving tackle by Stimpson at the end of the first half on Newcastle's Epi Taione kept the half-time score at 28-9.

Tigers returned hungry for more and within ten minutes a five-metre lineout gave the team a chance to capitalise on their

9 **Newcastle Falcons**

Pens: Wilkinson (3)

forwards' dominance with a catch and drive over the line for flanker Neil Back to burrow over.

Just five minutes later, exemplary support play and penetrating runs by both forwards and backs set up a powerful maul which drove Ollie Smith over the line to make the score 43-9.

Tigers were denied a further chance to score when Freddie Tuilagi made a storming run down the left wing, but a try-saving tackle forced the ball to spill just short of the line.

Graham Rowntree picked up the pace, making a series of piercing runs which eventually paid off with a fourth try for Tigers, which was also worth another bonus point in the Premiership.

Stimpson converted to make it 52-9 and complete a perfect personal haul of seven penalties, four conversions and a drop goal from 12 attempts.

Did you know?
Tigers' biggest ever league victory was against Newcastle Gosforth in 1994. Leicester beat the visitors 66-5 in the victory at Welford Road. Playing for Newcastle that day was Martin Corry.

Position	No.	Player
Full Back	15	L.Botham
Right Wing	14	J.Shaw
Centre	13	P.Godman
Centre	12	J.Noon
Left Wing	11	M.Stephenson
Fly Half	10	J.Wilkinson (c)
Scrum Half	9	J.Grindal
Prop	1	I.Peel
Hooker	2	S.Brotherstone
Prop	3	M.Hurter
Lock	4	H.Vyvyan
Lock	5	S.Grimes
Flanker	6	E.Taione
Flanker	7	R.Arnold
No.8	8	P.Dowson

Replacements: H.Charlton, R.Devonshire, C.Hamilton, J.Isaacson, M.Thompson, M.Ward, S.Otuvaka

Match Stats	LEICESTER TIGERS	NEWCASTLE FALCONS
Tackles	142	125
Missed Tackles	14	18
Ball Carries	82	81
Metres	591	443
Defenders Beaten	20	15
Passes	137	109
Clean Breaks	1	5
Pens / Free Kicks	13	12
Turnovers	14	16
Breakdowns Won	76	62
% Line-Outs Won	100	69
% Scrums Won	100	100

Bristol Shoguns 25

Tries: Christophers **Cons:** Contepomi
Pens: Contepomi (6)

Position	No.	Player
Full Back	15	L.Best
Right Wing	14	B.Daniel
Centre	13	M.Shaw
Centre	12	D.Gibson
Left Wing	11	P.Christophers
Fly Half	10	F.Contepomi
Scrum Half	9	A.Pichot
Prop	1	D.Crompton
Hooker	2	N.McCarthy
Prop	3	J.White
Lock	4	G.Archer (c)
Lock	5	A.Brown
Flanker	6	B.Sturnham
Flanker	7	M.Lipman
No.8	8	M.Salter

Replacements: E.Bergamaschi, S.Drahm, A.Higgins, P.Richards, A.Sheridan, C.Short, S.Nelson

Leicester Tigers narrowly lost out to bottom-placed Bristol Shoguns at the Memorial Stadium and notched up three away losses in a row.

Bristol were put at a disadvantage early on when prop Julian White was sent off for fighting at the scrum just 90 seconds into the game, but Tigers failed to take advantage of the one-man overlap and the home side took the lead nine minutes in with a well-taken Felipe Contepomi penalty.

Contepomi added three more penalties before Tigers opened their scoring with a storming Kafer try. Stimpson's conversion narrowed Tigers' deficit and we went into the half-time break five points down.

Stimpson was first to score in the second half with an easy three points which put Tigers within reach of their hosts, but a match-winning try by Phil Christophers, converted by Contepomi, took Bristol back out in front.

"We didn't capitalise after the sending off. It was all very disappointing."
– Dean Richards

20 Leicester Tigers

Tries: Kafer, Ellis   **Cons:** Stimpson (2)
Pens: Stimpson (2)

A Harry Ellis try couldn't save Tigers and Contepomi ended the visitors' chances with a further two penalties to take his match tally to 20 points and the final score to 25-20 to Bristol.

Position	No.	Player
Full Back	15	T.Stimpson
Right Wing	14	H.Ellis
Centre	13	O.Smith
Centre	12	R.Kafer
Left Wing	11	F.Tuilagi
Fly Half	10	S.Vesty
Scrum Half	9	T.Tierney
Prop	1	G.Rowntree
Hooker	2	D.West
Prop	3	D.Garforth
Lock	4	M.Johnson (c)
Lock	5	B.Kay
Flanker	6	M.Corry
Flanker	7	L.Moody
No.8	8	W.Johnson

Replacements: J.Naufahu, F.Tournaire, G.Chuter, G.Gelderbloom, J.Kronfeld, P.Short, S.Booth

Match Stats		
Tackles	124	79
Missed Tackles	23	20
Ball Carries	59	115
Metres	398	689
Defenders Beaten	16	23
Passes	93	148
Clean Breaks	5	6
Pens / Free Kicks	14	15
Turnovers	11	21
Breakdowns Won	48	87
% Line-Outs Won	72	92
% Scrums Won	92	100

September Review

Leicester Tigers took the good with the bad this month with an impressive home record but a disappointing away one. At home the team dominated the opposition, racking up some solid wins, 30-6 against NEC Harlequins and 52-9 against Newcastle Falcons.

However away from Welford Road, the side were unable to find their form and an injury-plagued start to the season saw Tigers suffer in the backs as the new season kicked off badly with a loss against Leeds Tykes at Headingley.

Ten Tigers were called up to Clive Woodward's England Elite squad to prepare for the autumn internationals against New Zealand, Australia and South Africa and the club welcomed its hottest new recruits – mascots Welford and JT – who became a firm favourite with the young supporters.

Off the field, the club's achievements were more notable and Welford Road was named as the most popular rugby venue in the UK by a Radio Five Live survey, beating national stadiums Twickenham and Murrayfield.

Snippets

Season ticket sales hit an all-time high with over 12,000 season tickets sold before the start of the season.

Tigers community department teamed up with the New Opportunities Fund (NOF) to work with 12 inner-city and special schools on a programme to develop coaching and interpersonal skills.

Results (Leicester Tigers' score first)

Aug 31	ZP	Leeds Tykes	A	3-26
Sept 7	ZP	NEC Harlequins	H	30-6
Sept 13	ZP	Sharks	A	16-29
Sept 21	ZP	Newcastle Falcons	H	52-9
Sept 29	ZP	Bristol Shoguns	A	20-25

Key

ZP	Zurich Premiership
ZW	Zurich Wildcard
HC	Heineken Cup
PGC	Powergen Cup

ZURICH PREMIERSHIP

Team	P	W	D	L	F	A	PD	BP	Pts
Gloucester	5	4	1	0	157	85	+72	2	20
London Wasps	5	3	1	1	164	130	+34	4	18
Leeds Tykes	5	3	1	1	149	108	+41	1	15
Northampton Saints	5	3	0	2	131	99	+32	2	14
Sharks	5	3	1	1	110	126	-16	0	14
Saracens	5	3	0	2	137	135	+2	1	13
Leicester Tigers	5	2	0	3	131	95	+36	3	1
Newcastle Falcons	5	2	0	3	92	142	-50	1	9
Bath Rugby	5	1	2	2	78	122	-44	0	8
London Irish	5	1	0	4	110	135	-25	2	6
NEC Harlequins	5	1	0	4	93	127	-34	2	6
Bristol Shoguns	5	1	0	4	136	184	-48	1	5

Top Points Scorers

Name	Total
T.Stimpson	73
N.Back	10
H.Ellis	10
R.Kafer	10
A.Healey	8
S.Booth	5

Top Try Scorers

Name	Total
H.Ellis	2
R.Kafer	2
N.Back	2
A.Healey	1
S.Booth	1
J.Hamilton	1

Player Of The Month

Tim Stimpson

Tim Stimpson continued his form from 2001/02 and kicked his way into the record books after achieving two Premiership records during this month.

He was presented with a Zurich Golden Boot award at the Sale game for scoring over 1,000 Premiership points and then equalled the Premiership's highest individual match score of 32 points when Tigers faced Newcastle just a week later.

The international back scored an awesome 63 points for Tigers during September which was his highest monthly score of the season.

Appearances	5
Tackles	17
Misses	6
Ball Carries	43
Metres	371
Passes	20
Defenders Beaten	8
Clean Breaks	3
Points Scored	73
Bombs Defused	3

Top Penalty Scorers

Name	Total
T.Stimpson	15

Top Drop Goal Scorers

Name	Tries
T.Stimpson	1
A.Healey	1

Regular season matches only

Leicester Tigers   22

Tries: Back, Corry, West **Cons:** Stimpson (2)
Pens: Stimpson

Position	No.	Player
Full Back	15	T.Stimpson
Right Wing	14	S.Booth
Centre	13	L.Lloyd
Centre	12	R.Kafer
Left Wing	11	F.Tuilagi
Fly Half	10	A.Healey
Scrum Half	9	T.Tierney
Prop	1	G.Rowntree
Hooker	2	D.West
Prop	3	F.Tournaire
Lock	4	M.Johnson (c)
Lock	5	L.Deacon
Flanker	6	L.Moody
Flanker	7	N.Back
No.8	8	M.Corry

Replacements: G.Chuter, D.Garforth, G.Gelderbloom, J.Hamilton, W.Johnson, B.Kay, J.Kronfeld

In notching up their 50th successive home win Leicester Tigers gave the sell-out crowd a scare in a 22-20 thriller against old rivals Bath. The unbeaten run in the Zurich Premiership after the hard fought match stretched back as far as December 1997.

> "It has been tough and it's going to be just as tough in Europe because we travel to Neath on Friday." – **Dean Richards**

The gruelling encounter saw six changes from the side that had lost to Bristol the previous week – including the return of Austin Healey after injury at fly-half. Bath were strengthened by the return of international Mike Catt who appeared to dominate the early play, resulting in a difficult touchline penalty being converted by Olly Barkley. Bath remained on top and left Tigers, who had most of the possession, frustrated as they continually thwarted the home sides' attempts to score. Barkley converted another penalty and Tim Stimpson missed two. But Tigers still pressed forward, eager to make amends before the break.

Their patience was well rewarded with a Healey kick to the left corner being flicked on by Neil Back to Martin Corry who pounced on the ball and scored. Tigers remained 5-6 behind going into the second half.

Tim Stimpson returned from the break with his kicking boots on, landing an impressive penalty from five metres in his own half next to the touchline. Tigers were making all the moves and taking control of the game with the majority of possession but somehow this was not translated into points, with Healey being held up over

20

Bath Rugby

Tries: Maggs, Tindall   **Cons:** Barkley (2)
Pens: Barkley (2)

the line. The frustration was beginning to show as scrum-half Tom Tierney received a warning from the referee for illegal use of the boot. Eventually the tide turned and Tigers forwards seized the moment and broke away from the Bath defence, Tim Stimpson converting a try by hooker Dorian West.

Mike Catt received a yellow card shortly after for a straight arm tackle on Martin Corry and Tigers were quick to capitalise. Neil Back scored a typical try from the maul, and Stimpson added the conversion. With the score at 25-6 Tigers appeared to take their foot of the gas - surely an easy win was in sight.

The sin-binning of Austin Healey and substitute flanker James Scaysbrook combined with two tries scored in quick succession in the closing minutes of the game from Kevin Maggs and Mike Tindall, ensured that the Welford Road faithful were left on the edge of their seats until the referee Dave Pearson finally blew the whistle.

Did you know?
Scoring 7 points in this game, Tim Stimpson surpassed John Liley's record of 119 points in 15 games, having scored the same in 9 games against Bath.

Position	No.	Player
Full Back	15	O.Barkley
Right Wing	14	S.Danielli
Centre	13	M.Tindall
Centre	12	K.Maggs
Left Wing	11	T.Voyce
Fly Half	10	M.Catt
Scrum Half	9	G.Cooper
Prop	1	D.Barnes
Hooker	2	J.Humphreys
Prop	3	A.Galasso
Lock	4	A.Beattie
Lock	5	D.Grewcock (c)
Flanker	6	G.Thomas
Flanker	7	D.Lyle
No.8	8	N.Thomas

Replacements: R.Blake, J.Scayesbrook, A.Lloyd, J.Mallett, C.Malone, L.Mears, A.Crockett

Match Stats	TIGERS	BATH RUGBY
Tackles	113	138
Missed Tackles	14	15
Ball Carries	79	68
Metres	519	398
Defenders Beaten	11	16
Passes	127	85
Clean Breaks	4	0
Pens / Free Kicks	9	16
Turnovers	7	7
Breakdowns Won	77	65
% Line-Outs Won	86	81
% Scrums Won	82	67

Neath

16

Tries: Tiueti **Cons:** Jarvis
Pens: Jarvis (3)

Position	No.	Player
Full Back	15	G.Morris
Right Wing	14	K.James
Centre	13	J.Storey
Centre	12	D.Tiueti
Left Wing	11	S.Williams
Fly Half	10	L.Jarvis
Scrum Half	9	A.Moore
Prop	1	D.Jones
Hooker	2	B.Williams
Prop	3	A.Millward
Lock	4	A.Newman
Lock	5	G.Llewellyn (c)
Flanker	6	H.Jenkins
Flanker	7	A.Mocelutu
No.8	8	N.Bonner-Evans

Replacements: S.Connor, P.Horgan, A.Jones, S.Jones, S.Martin, S.Tandy

Tigers kicked off their Heineken Cup campaign poorly against Neath with a 16-16 draw at The Gnoll.

The first half was as miserable as the weather with the driving rain slowing down play and forcing errors on both sides.

Poor discipline let Tigers down and allowed Neath to take a 13-3 half-time lead courtesy of Lee Jarvis' boot and Dave Tiueti's turn of pace.

A frustrated Tigers side upped the tempo in the second half and threatened Neath's line on a number of occasions, but they were unable to cross and reverted to kicking with Tim Stimpson slotting two penalties through the posts.

> "I don't like to have a go at refs so I won't. But the game was lost on a decision that was far from agreeable."
> **– Austin Healey**

Two missed penalties within two minutes stopped Tigers' closing the gap further and they had to wait until the 79th minute to add another score.

In a moment of inspiration, Austin Healey dug Tigers out of a hole as he has done in so many vital fixtures before. Healey cleared the ball from his own 22 to land deep in the Neath half. The resulting line-out was knocked on to give Tigers an attacking scrum within good distance of the line.

The speedy fly half ran across the field and dummied the Welsh defence to take the ball over the line in the corner and score near the posts. Stimpson converted, giving Tigers a three-point lead.

Tigers fought to keep the home side out of their 22 from the restart but the pressure showed and Tigers prop Franck Tournaire cracked to give away a penalty within range of the posts for Jarvis to level the scores in the final minute.

16 Leicester Tigers

Tries: Healey **Cons:** Stimpson
Pens: Stimpson (3)

Did you know?
Leicester first played Neath in 1908 winning 9-8 at Welford Road.

Match Stats		
Tackles	159	59
Missed Tackles	27	8
Ball Carries	27	80
Metres	112	455
Defenders Beaten	9	25
Passes	42	118
Clean Breaks	0	2
Pens / Free Kicks	11	12
Turnovers	8	14
Breakdowns Won	36	74
% Line-Outs Won	82	86
% Scrums Won	90	90

Position	No.	Player
Full Back	15	T.Stimpson
Right Wing	14	L.Lloyd
Centre	13	G.Gelderbloom
Centre	12	R.Kafer
Left Wing	11	F.Tuilagi
Fly Half	10	A.Healey
Scrum Half	9	T.Tierney
Prop	1	G.Rowntree
Hooker	2	D.West
Prop	3	D.Garforth
Lock	4	M.Johnson (c)
Lock	5	B.Kay
Flanker	6	L.Moody
Flanker	7	N.Back
No.8	8	M.Corry

Replacements: G.Chuter, P.Freshwater, F.Tournaire, W.Johnson, S.Booth, J.Kronfeld, Jamie Hamilton

Leicester Tigers 63

Tries: Freshwater, Corry, Back (2), Tierney, Booth (3), Murphy (2)
Cons: Murphy, Stimpson (3), Healey **Pens:** Healey

Position	No.	Player
Full Back	15	G.Murphy
Right Wing	14	A.Healey
Centre	13	L.Lloyd
Centre	12	R.Kafer
Left Wing	11	S.Booth
Fly Half	10	S.Vesty
Scrum Half	9	T.Tierney
Prop	1	P.Freshwater
Hooker	2	G.Chuter
Prop	3	F.Tournaire
Lock	4	L.Deacon
Lock	5	M.Corry
Flanker	6	J.Kronfeld
Flanker	7	N.Back (c)
No.8	8	W.Johnson

Replacements: A.Balding, D.Garforth, G.Gelderbloom, J.Hamilton, M.Johnson, T.Stimpson, D.West

Tigers' opening home game of the Heineken Cup saw some of the magic that crowned the team back-to-back European Champions.

Tigers were keen to make an impression early on and within 15 minutes a break by full back Geordan Murphy set up Steve Booth to score in the corner.

Calvisano tried to equalise with two drop goal attempts but both kicks by number 10, Giovanni Raineri, went wide of the posts.

Thirty minutes into the half, a cocky penalty kick by winger Austin Healey from just inside the Calvisano half spun through the posts to give Tigers an 8-0 lead.

> "It was a no-win situation for us as people expected us to win and win well."
> – Dean Richards

The last 10 minutes of the half saw the home side pick up their game with three further tries and a conversion. The first came from Neil Back in a trademark catch and drive from just five metres out.

⬜ Amatori & Calvisano

Perry Freshwater was next to score after an outstanding break by Steve Booth and run by fellow front-rower George Chuter.

In the last minute of the half, Geordan Murphy made an inspirational break from his own 22, dodging the Calvisano defence and offloading to Booth who fell short of the line. The lightning full back recycled himself to take a pop from hooker George Chuter, and dived over the line to score his first try of the season. A conversion by Healey made the half time score 25-0.

The Tigers side returned in the second half hungry for more points, with a try after just two minutes by scrum half Tom Tierney. Calvisano barely got a look-in as a confident Tigers team steamrolled the visiting side. Further tries from Neil Back, Geordan Murphy, Martin Corry and Steve Booth (who completed his hat-trick), added to four conversions by Tim Stimpson and Geordan Murphy.

Position	No.	Player
Full Back	15	M.Ravazzolo
Right Wing	14	P.Vaccari
Centre	13	M.Gabba
Centre	12	C.Zanoletti
Left Wing	11	E.Muliero
Fly Half	10	G.Raineri
Scrum Half	9	J.Dragotto
Prop	1	D.Davo
Hooker	2	A.Moretti
Prop	3	G.De Carli (c)
Lock	4	L.Mastrodomencio
Lock	5	W.Boardman
Flanker	6	C.Mayerhofler
Flanker	7	R.Mandelli
No.8	8	A.De Rossi

Replacements: S.Ciampa, G.Bocca, J.Purll, C.Roux, P.Griffen, S.Varella

Did you know?
This game saw Tigers centre Glenn Gelderbloom make his 50th appearance for the club, since his debut in the Cardiff pre-season game in 2001.

Match Stats	LEICESTER TIGERS	⭐
Tackles	103	128
Missed Tackles	12	40
Ball Carries	131	76
Metres	1044	212
Defenders Beaten	38	10
Passes	167	100
Clean Breaks	27	2
Pens / Free Kicks	13	14
Turnovers	22	15
Breakdowns Won	59	52
% Line-Outs Won	85	76
% Scrums Won	100	82

ZURICH
PREMIERSHIP

Date: **Sunday 27th October 2002**

Saracens   18

Tries: Shanklin, Castaignede **Cons:** Goode
Pens: Goode (2)

Position	No.	Player
Full Back	15	T.Castaignede
Right Wing	14	T.Shanklin
Centre	13	K.Sorrell
Centre	12	T.Horan
Left Wing	11	D.O'Mahony
Fly Half	10	A.Goode
Scrum Half	9	K.Bracken (c)
Prop	1	C.Califano
Hooker	2	M.Cairns
Prop	3	J.Marsters
Lock	4	S.Hooper
Lock	5	C.Yandell
Flanker	6	K.Chesney
Flanker	7	A.Roques
No.8	8	R.Hill

Replacements: A.Benazzi, D.Flatman,
B.Johnston, A.Kershaw, C.Quinnell,
M.Williams, A.Winnan

Tigers clinched their first Premiership away win of the season against Saracens in a tight match at Vicarage Road.

Tigers were first to open the scoring with a Tim Stimpson penalty following an infringement at the breakdown.

It took ex-Tiger Andy Goode four shots at the posts to level the scores after three early misses at goal.

Stimpson replied to put Tigers back in the lead. However, it was short-lived as Saracens wing Tom Shanklin intercepted a Leicester attack to cross the visitors' line for the first try of the game on the 30 minute mark.

> "It might have been totally different had Andy Goode kicked all his goals but thankfully he missed." – **Dean Richards**

Unsurprisingly, Goode missed the conversion and Stimpson kicked his third penalty as Tigers went into the break with a narrow 9-8 lead.

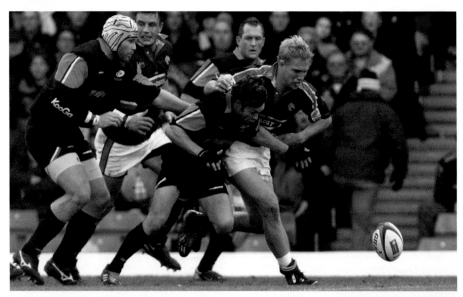

26   Leicester Tigers

Tries: Booth, Murphy **Cons:** Stimpson (2)
Pens: Stimpson (3) **DGs:** Murphy

Straight from the kick off, Tigers were back in command and speedy winger Steve Booth scampered over in the first minute, with Stimpson adding the extras, to increase the visitors' lead.

The second half continued in the same see-saw fashion as the first and less than ten minutes later Saracens were back in contention when Castaignede made the most of a Martin Corry sin binning to dart over for the home side's second try of the afternoon. Goode converted to bring the men in black back within a point of Tigers.

It was then Ireland international Geordan Murphy's turn to take command with a try in the 72nd minute. Stimpson converted and Murphy sealed the victory on the final whistle with a well-timed drop goal, denying Saracens a bonus point and securing Tigers' first away victory of the season, 26-18.

Did you know?
This game was Tigers' fourth Premiership win in a row against Saracens.

Position	No.	Player
Full Back	15	T.Stimpson
Right Wing	14	G.Murphy
Centre	13	L.Lloyd
Centre	12	R.Kafer
Left Wing	11	S.Booth
Fly Half	10	S.Vesty
Scrum Half	9	T.Tierney
Prop	1	G.Rowntree
Hooker	2	G.Chuter
Prop	3	D.Garforth
Lock	4	M.Johnson (c)
Lock	5	B.Kay
Flanker	6	L.Moody
Flanker	7	N.Back
No.8	8	M.Corry

Replacements: P.Freshwater, D.West, G.Gelderbloom, J.Hamilton, J.Kronfeld, C.McMullen, F.Tournaire

Match Stats	SARACENS	LEICESTER TIGERS
Tackles	136	62
Missed Tackles	21	22
Ball Carries	66	103
Metres	460	653
Defenders Beaten	18	24
Passes	105	122
Clean Breaks	5	0
Pens / Free Kicks	8	12
Turnovers	10	10
Breakdowns Won	47	86
% Line-Outs Won	75	92
% Scrums Won	71	100

October Review

October saw a dramatic improvement for Tigers and the team won three and drew one match during this period. The month kicked off with a win over Bath which took Tigers to an amazing 50 successive Premiership wins in a row at Welford Road.

October also marked the start of the Heineken Cup pool matches and Tigers drew with Neath at The Gnoll before giving Amatori & Calvisano a 63-0 drubbing at Welford Road the following week.

Tigers announced a new signing in the form of lightning rugby league winger, Gareth Raynor, who joined the club from Hull FC at the end of the Super League season.

Away from the field, Tigers teamed up with LOROS to raise money through the sale of small cuddly Tigers with all profits going direct to the charity. To date, the club has raised over £3,000 which has been ploughed into hospice care in the Leicestershire area.

Snippets

Tigers hold a celebration dinner in recognition of the club's success over the last four years. Ex-Tigers and British Lions player, Sir Tony O'Reilly, was the guest speaker for over 500 guests.

The Prima Tiger Cup was launched at Vipers RFC on Oct 6. The U10s competition started with a knockout tournament with winners playing in quarter-finals at Welford Road.

Results (Leicester Tigers' score first)

Oct 5	ZP	Bath Rugby	H	22-20
Oct 11	HC	Neath	A	16-16
Oct 19	HC	Amatori & Calvisano	H	63-0
Oct 27	ZP	Saracens	A	26-18

Key

ZP	Zurich Premiership
ZW	Zurich Wildcard
HC	Heineken Cup
PGC	Powergen Cup

ZURICH PREMIERSHIP

Team	P	W	D	L	F	A	PD	BP	Pts
Gloucester	7	5	1	1	217	122	+95	4	26
Leeds Tykes	7	5	1	1	196	141	+55	1	23
Northampton Saints	7	5	0	2	179	131	+48	2	22
London Wasps	7	4	1	2	207	180	+27	4	22
Leicester Tigers	7	4	0	3	179	133	+46	3	19
Sharks	7	4	1	2	166	171	-5	1	19
Newcastle Falcons	7	3	0	4	146	209	-63	2	14
Saracens	7	3	0	4	169	205	-36	1	13
NEC Harlequins	6	2	0	4	140	150	-10	3	11
Bath Rugby	7	1	2	4	118	166	-48	2	10
London Irish	7	1	0	6	136	185	-49	3	7
Bristol Shoguns	6	1	0	5	149	209	-60	1	5

October Review

Top Points Scorers

Name	Total
T.Stimpson	93
N.Back	15
S.Booth	10
H.Ellis	10
R.Kafer	10
G.Murphy	8

Top Try Scorers

Name	Total
N.Back	3
S.Booth	2
H.Ellis	2
R.Kafer	2
M.Corry	1
D.West	1

Top Penalty Scorers

Name	Total
T.Stimpson	19

Top Drop Goal Scorers

Name	Total
G.Murphy	1
T.Stimpson	1
A.Healey	1

Regular season matches only

 Player Of The Month

Martin Corry

Martin's versatility in the pack earned him the October Lumbers Player of the Month Award. Starting every game, he scored ten points for Tigers to see the club unbeaten all month.

Appearances	2
Tackles	14
Missed Tackles	5
Ball Carries	19
Metres	91
Clean Breaks	0
Defenders Beaten	1
Lineouts Won	8
Tries Scored	1

Leicester Tigers   9

Pens: Stimpson (3)

Position	No.	Player
Full Back	15	T.Stimpson
Right Wing	14	G.Murphy
Centre	13	L.Lloyd
Centre	12	G.Gelderbloom
Left Wing	11	S.Booth
Fly Half	10	S.Vesty
Scrum Half	9	J.Hamilton
Prop	1	P.Freshwater
Hooker	2	D.West
Prop	3	D.Garforth
Lock	4	M.Johnson (c)
Lock	5	B.Kay
Flanker	6	J.Kronfeld
Flanker	7	N.Back
No.8	8	M.Corry

Replacements: A.Balding, F.Tournaire, W.Johnson, C.McMullen, J.Naufahu, P.Short, G.Chuter

Tigers beat London Wasps in front of a full house at a rain-soaked Welford Road.

The game opened well for Tigers. Winger Geordan Murphy kicked off and within a minute Leicester had regained possession. A high kick from Murphy set Tigers up five metres from the Wasps line but the enthusiastic side were called up for crossing by the referee.

The exciting start was short-lived, and after eight minutes Wasps fly half Mark van Gisbergen kicked a penalty to give the visitors an early lead.

The wet weather didn't help consistency of play and both teams opted to kick for territory. Ten minutes after the first points went on the board, Tim Stimpson equalised with a penalty.

Two Stimpson penalties later and a further kick from van Gisbergen left the half-time score at 9-6 to Tigers.

"I'm just glad that we came away with a victory because the conditions out there were atrocious." – **Dean Richards**

6

London Wasps

Pens: van Gisbergen (2)

As the light rain turned into a mist in the second half Tigers continued to dominate the match, but the poor weather forced mistakes on both sides. A number of opportunities were missed by Tigers and the team were closed down by a strong Wasps defence.

Tigers regained momentum into the third quarter with some exciting passages of play, but the team was unable to capitalise on a number of opportunities including a four on two overlap down the left wing.

Wasps stepped up their game in the final quarter, helped by a string of tactical substitutions including bringing Rob Howley on at scrum half. His arrival changed Wasps' direction of play and the home team were tested when a poor decision by Gelderbloom saw the ball slide from deep inside the Wasps half to just five metres from Tigers' try line with strong pressure from Howley.

Tigers managed to hold Wasps back in the second half but were stopped from putting points on the board themselves. Both sides were unable to score from attempts at goal to leave the second half scoreless and the final result 9-6 to Tigers.

Position	No.	Player
Full Back	15	P.Sampson
Right Wing	14	J.Rudd
Centre	13	M.Denney
Centre	12	F.Waters
Left Wing	11	J.Lewsey
Fly Half	10	M.van Gisbergen
Scrum Half	9	M.Wood
Prop	1	C.Dowd
Hooker	2	T.Leota
Prop	3	D.Molloy
Lock	4	S.Shaw
Lock	5	J.Beardshaw
Flanker	6	L.Dallaglio (c)
Flanker	7	P.Volley
No.8	8	P.Scrivener

Replacements: S.Abbott, R.Birkett B.Gotting, W.Green, R.Howley, M.Lock, K.Logan

Match Stats	TIGERS	WASPS
Tackles	107	87
Missed Tackles	7	15
Ball Carries	59	72
Metres	284	340
Defenders Beaten	14	9
Passes	79	67
Clean Breaks	0	0
Pens / Free Kicks	9	14
Turnovers	15	12
Breakdowns Won	61	56
% Line-Outs Won	75	68
% Scrums Won	80	100

Northampton Saints   3

Pens: Grayson

Position	No.	Player
Full Back	15	N.Beal
Right Wing	14	J.Sleightholme
Centre	13	M.Tucker
Centre	12	J.Leslie (c)
Left Wing	11	O.Ripol
Fly Half	10	P.Grayson
Scrum Half	9	J.Howard
Prop	1	R.Morris
Hooker	2	D.Richmond
Prop	3	C.Budgen
Lock	4	J.Phillips
Lock	5	M.Connors
Flanker	6	G.Seely
Flanker	7	A.Blowers
No.8	8	M.Soden

Replacements: J.Brooks, R.Hunter, M.Miles, B.Reihana, B.Sturgess, I.Vass, D.Fox

Leicester Tigers were back on track as they beat East Midlands rivals Northampton 16-3 at Franklin's Gardens.

With six players on international duty, Tigers' strength and depth shone through with the only try of the game coming from former All Black Josh Kronfeld, who crossed the line in the second half from a typical Tigers driving maul from a lineout.

Tigers started well and it was only four minutes into the game that the vistors scored the first three points from a Geordan Murphy boot.

Northampton fly half Paul Grayson kicked the home side's only points before the break with Murphy taking his penalty tally to three and Tigers' half-time lead to 9-3.

Tigers outperformed the Saints in the second half with the home side rarely stepping into Leicester territory.

The Kronfeld try came 10 minutes from time with Murphy adding the extras to firm up Tigers' lead and leave the final score at 16-3.

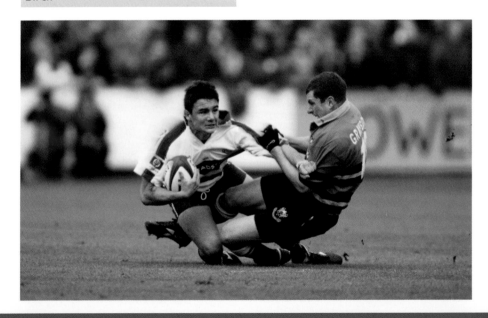

16 Leicester Tigers

Tries: Kronfeld   **Cons:** Murphy
Pens: Murphy (3)

"We struggled a little bit early on in the season but we are starting to get into the swing of things." – **Dean Richards**

Match Stats		
Tackles	100	132
Missed Tackles	13	15
Ball Carries	87	88
Metres	555	344
Defenders Beaten	10	10
Passes	116	93
Clean Breaks	4	0
Pens / Free Kicks	16	13
Turnovers	23	12
Breakdowns Won	81	68
% Line-Outs Won	68	88
% Scrums Won	89	100

Position	No.	Player
Full Back	15	G.Murphy
Right Wing	14	L.Lloyd
Centre	13	O.Smith
Centre	12	R.Kafer
Left Wing	11	S.Booth
Fly Half	10	C.McMullen
Scrum Half	9	H.Ellis
Prop	1	P.Freshwater
Hooker	2	D.West (c)
Prop	3	F.Tournaire
Lock	4	L.Deacon
Lock	5	M.Corry
Flanker	6	W.Johnson
Flanker	7	J.Kronfeld
No.8	8	A.Balding

Replacements: G.Chuter, D.Garforth, G.Gelderbloom, B.Gerry, J.Hamilton, P.Short, S.Vesty

Date: Friday 15th November 200

Leicester Tigers 2C

Tries: Lloyd, Kronfeld (2)
Cons: Vesty **Pens:** Vesty

Position	No.	Player
Full Back	15	L.Lloyd
Right Wing	14	F.Tuilagi
Centre	13	O.Smith
Centre	12	R.Kafer
Left Wing	11	S.Booth
Fly Half	10	S.Vesty
Scrum Half	9	H.Ellis
Prop	1	P.Freshwater
Hooker	2	D.West (c)
Prop	3	D.Garforth
Lock	4	L.Deacon
Lock	5	M.Corry
Flanker	6	W.Johnson
Flanker	7	J.Kronfeld
No.8	8	A.Balding

Replacements: G.Chuter, G.Gelderbloom, B.Gerry, G.Raynor, P.Short, T.Tierney, F.Tournaire

Premiership leaders Gloucester made it clear to capacity Welford Road stadium that they mea business with a try after just one minute courte of openside flanker, Jake Boer.

The game restarted with Tigers hungry to p points on the board and their opportunity came aft eight minutes with a Sam Vesty penalty in front the posts to bring the score to 5-3.

A free kick after ten minutes saw Vesty spin t ball into the Gloucester half for a Tigers line-out the ten-metre line. Gloucester were quick to cle but an early tackle on Freddie Tuilagi by Marc Garvey gave Tigers a penalty from which Sam Ves produced a carbon copy of the previous kick resulti in another Tigers line-out.

A clear catch by Martin Corry set up a drive Perry Freshwater and a frantic ball shot down t back line to Steve Booth, who fixed the defence wi a trademark scamper for full back Leon Lloyd steam down the wing and dive over in the corner.

Tigers continued to put pressure on the visito and the team made a number of breaks through t Gloucester half but with no score.

15   # Gloucester

Tries: Boer, Fanolua **Cons:** Paul
Pens: Paul

It was lack of discipline by Gloucester that gave Tigers the advantage and allowed them to score two almost identical Josh Kronfeld tries from a drive and dive over the line. Vesty converted one try to bring the half-time score to 20-5.

> "A lot of people have written us off at their peril." – **Dean Richards**

It was stalemate in the second half with no score until the 34th minute. The fierce battle continued as Gloucester regained some discipline and were the only side to put points on the board.

Despite an injured Marcel Garvey being stretchered off the field, the visitors were able to steal a try and add a conversion and penalty to their single score in the first half.

However, Gloucester's lucky points weren't enough to steal the game, giving Tigers a well deserved 20-15 win.

Position	No.	Player
Full Back	15	H.Paul
Right Wing	14	M.Garvey
Centre	13	T.Fanolua
Centre	12	R.Todd
Left Wing	11	T.Delport
Fly Half	10	L.Mercier
Scrum Half	9	C.Stuart-Smith
Prop	1	R.Roncero
Hooker	2	O.Azam
Prop	3	A.Deacon
Lock	4	A.Eustace
Lock	5	M.Cornwell
Flanker	6	P.Buxton
Flanker	7	J.Boer (c)
No.8	8	J.Paramore

Replacements: J.Forrester, M.Irish, C.Catling, R.Elloway, R.Fidler, J.Frape, T.Beim

Match Stats	LEICESTER TIGERS	GLOUCESTER RFC
Tackles	57	118
Missed Tackles	13	16
Ball Carries	84	56
Metres	295	266
Defenders Beaten	12	18
Passes	74	73
Clean Breaks	7	0
Pens / Free Kicks	9	19
Turnovers	13	11
Breakdowns Won	77	43
% Line-Outs Won	89	74
% Scrums Won	67	73

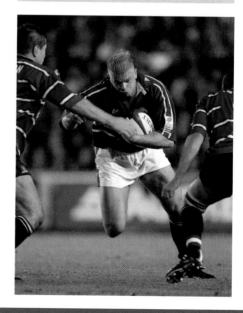

London Irish 27

Tries: Horak, Everitt **Cons:** Everitt
Pens: Everitt (4) **DGs:** Everitt

Position	No.	Player
Full Back	15	M.Horak
Right Wing	14	P.Sackey
Centre	13	N.Burrows
Centre	12	B.Venter
Left Wing	11	P.Rossouw
Fly Half	10	B.Everitt
Scrum Half	9	D.Edwards
Prop	1	M.Worsley
Hooker	2	N.Drotske
Prop	3	R.Hardwick
Lock	4	R.Strudwick (c)
Lock	5	N.Kennedy
Flanker	6	P.Gustard
Flanker	7	D.Danagher
No.8	8	C.Sheasby

Replacements: K.Barrett, J.Cockle, G.Delaney, A.Flavin, S.Halford, N.Hatley, M.Mapletoft

Leicester Tigers' winning streak was brought to a grinding halt at a rain-soaked Madejski Stadium with the reigning Premiership champions losing 27-7 to bottom-placed London Irish.

Although Tigers suffered with nine internationals away on duty, it was their lack of a dominant kicker that lost them the game.

The Exiles were first to score with fly half Barry Everitt nudging the ball over twice before Tigers could put any points on the board. Tigers then scored the opening try from a line-out deep in the Irish half.

Sam Vesty spun the ball out for centre Ollie Smith who stormed over the line. Steve Booth converted to take Tigers into the lead at the break 7-6.

The second half was as dismal as the weather for Tigers, who failed to add to their seven-point scoreline. London Irish made the most of the solid Everitt boot with two more penalties and a drop goal adding to their second half tally.

"We are not pressing the panic buttons just yet." – **Dean Richards**

7 Leicester Tigers

Tries: Smith
Cons: Booth

Any chance of a Tigers comeback was wiped out in injury time when Irish ran in two tries from Everitt and Michael Horak. Everitt converted one to take his personal tally to 22 and the final score to 27-7 to Irish.

Match Stats		
Tackles	150	66
Missed Tackles	19	7
Ball Carries	49	124
Metres	255	430
Defenders Beaten	5	25
Passes	67	107
Clean Breaks	1	7
Pens / Free Kicks	11	15
Turnovers	13	17
Breakdowns Won	42	96
% Line-Outs Won	86	75
% Scrums Won	100	100

Position	No.	Player
Full Back	15	L.Lloyd
Right Wing	14	S.Booth
Centre	13	O.Smith
Centre	12	R.Kafer
Left Wing	11	F.Tuilagi
Fly Half	10	S.Vesty
Scrum Half	9	H.Ellis
Prop	1	P.Freshwater
Hooker	2	D.West (c)
Prop	3	D.Garforth
Lock	4	L.Deacon
Lock	5	M.Corry
Flanker	6	P.Short
Flanker	7	J.Kronfeld
No.8	8	A.Balding

Replacements: G.Chuter, G.Gelderbloom, B.Gerry, G.Raynor, T.Tierney, F.Tournaire, B.Wheeler

Leicester Tigers   12

Pens: Stimpson (4)

Position	No.	Player
Full Back	15	T.Stimpson
Right Wing	14	G.Murphy
Centre	13	O.Smith
Centre	12	R.Kafer
Left Wing	11	F.Tuilagi
Fly Half	10	A.Healey
Scrum Half	9	H.Ellis
Prop	1	G.Rowntree
Hooker	2	G.Chuter
Prop	3	F.Tournaire
Lock	4	M.Johnson (c)
Lock	5	B.Kay
Flanker	6	M.Corry
Flanker	7	J.Kronfeld
No.8	8	W.Johnson

Replacements: B.Gerry, P.Freshwater, J.Buckland, A.Balding, S.Booth, L.Lloyd, T.Tierney

Leicester Tigers' Welford Road winning streak came to a dramatic end with a defeat by East Midlands rivals Northampton Saints.

Despite a promising start by the home team and some big hits which saw Northampton scrum half Matt Dawson stretchered off, Tigers weren't able to score past the strong Northampton defence.

A clever five metre line-out move after 25 minutes allowed Northampton captain Budge Pountney to take the ball blind and score in the corner, with Paul Grayson converting.

> "Our achievement pales compared to what Leicester have built here in the last few years."
> **– Paul Grayson, Northampton Saints**

Tigers fought back and a penalty after 39 minutes put Tim Stimpson in the record books as only the third Leicester player to score 1,500 points for the club, leaving the half-time score at 13-6 to Northampton.

The second half started well for Tigers who were gifted three points after just three minutes. This was quickly followed by a yellow card for Northampton lock Rob Hunter following an infringement at a rolling maul, giving Tigers a one-man overlap.

A second Stimpson penalty closed the gap to just one point and Tigers looked like they were on the verge of turning the score around with strong back play by Harry Ellis and Freddie Tuilagi.

The half continued with no score for Tigers and Northampton took advantage of Tigers' poor defence when a gap on the blind side of the ruck allowed Ian Vass to shuttle down the wing and score unopposed in the corner.

25 Northampton Saints

Tries: Pountney, Vass, Hyndman
Cons: Grayson (2) **Pens:** Grayson (2)

A third try from centre Chris Hyndman less than ten minutes later put the nails in the Tigers coffin, to leave the final score at 25-12 to Northampton.

Position	No.	Player
Full Back	15	N.Beal
Right Wing	14	B.Reihana
Centre	13	C.Hyndman
Centre	12	J.Leslie
Left Wing	11	B.Cohen
Fly Half	10	P.Grayson
Scrum Half	9	M.Dawson
Prop	1	T.Smith
Hooker	2	S.Thompson
Prop	3	C.Budgen
Lock	4	M.Lord
Lock	5	R.Hunter
Flanker	6	A.Blowers
Flanker	7	B.Pountney (c)
No.8	8	M.Soden

Replacements: D.Richmond, R.Morris, J.Phillips, S.Hepher, I.Vass, J.Brooks, J.Sleightholme

Match Stats		
Tackles	55	147
Missed Tackles	4	17
Ball Carries	111	38
Metres	306	219
Defenders Beaten	17	9
Passes	136	60
Clean Breaks	2	3
Pens / Free Kicks	9	11
Turnovers	17	20
Breakdowns Won	96	36
% Line-Outs Won	84	71
% Scrums Won	93	100

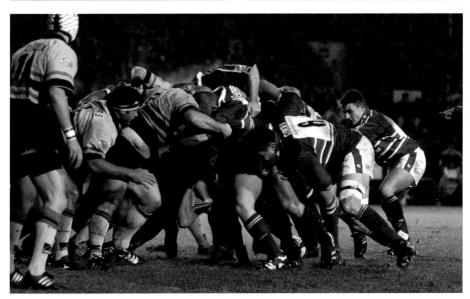

November Review

This jam packed month had five Premiership fixtures crammed into it starting with a try-less match against London Wasps on November 7.

Tigers were on a winning streak and notched up seven wins in a row, winning their first three games of the month, the highlight being a 20-15 win over league leaders Gloucester at Welford Road.

The high came too soon and Tigers lost the following week to London Irish at the Madejski Stadium before hitting a low at the end of the month when they lost their undefeated home record to local rivals, Northampton Saints.

Off the field, November was a particularly good month for the Tigers community department who were recognised at the 2002 Sportsmatch Awards for their outstanding Alliance & Leicester Tag programme. Tigers were awarded the top 'Overall Sportsmatch Programme of 2002' for the work of their four-strong community team. The club was also nominated for and won the 'Best Schools Sport Programme'.

Snippets

Leicester Tigers community department are presented with a Land Rover Discovery in recognition of their hard work.

Tigers and BBC Radio Leicester raise over £3,600 for Children In Need at the Gloucester match with bucket collections, half-time kicking fun and a pre-match mascot race.

Results (Leicester Tigers' score first)

Date	Comp	Opponent	H/A	Score
Nov 2	ZP	London Wasps	H	9-6
Nov 9	ZP	Northampton Saints	A	16-3
Nov 15	ZP	Gloucester	H	20-15
Nov 24	ZP	London Irish	A	7-27
Nov 30	ZP	Northampton Saints	H	12-25

Key

ZP	Zurich Premiership
ZW	Zurich Wildcard
HC	Heineken Cup
PGC	Powergen Cup

ZURICH PREMIERSHIP

Team	P	W	D	L	F	A	PD	BP	Pts
Gloucester	12	9	1	2	343	200	+143	6	44
Sharks	12	8	1	3	317	278	+39	5	39
Leeds Tykes	12	7	2	3	301	251	+50	2	34
Northampton Saints	12	7	0	5	270	210	+60	4	32
Leicester Tigers	12	7	0	5	243	209	+34	3	31
London Wasps	12	5	2	5	297	290	+7	6	30
NEC Harlequins	11	5	0	6	258	276	-18	5	25
Saracens	12	5	0	7	298	348	-50	4	24
Bristol Shoguns	11	4	1	6	283	310	-27	3	21
London Irish	12	3	1	8	258	305	-47	4	18
Bath Rugby	12	3	2	7	212	288	-76	2	18
Newcastle Falcons	12	3	0	9	217	332	-115	4	16

Top Points Scorers

Name	Total
T.Stimpson	114
G.Murphy	19
J.Kronfeld	15
N.Back	15
S.Booth	12
O.Smith	10

Top Try Scorers

Name	Total
J.Kronfeld	3
O.Smith	2
N.Back	2
S.Booth	2
H.Ellis	2
R.Kafer	2

Top Penalty Scorers

Name	Total
T.Stimpson	26
G.Murphy	3
S.Vesty	1

Top Drop Goal Scorers

Name	Total
G.Murphy	1
T.Stimpson	1
A.Healey	1

Regular season matches only

 Player Of The Month

Josh Kronfeld

Appearances	4
Tackles	43
Missed Tackles	5
Tackle Success %	91
Ball Carries	42
Metres	169
Defenders Beaten	6
Turnovers Won	4
Tries Scored	3
Average Gain Per Carry	4m

Josh really made his mark in November and was named as the Zurich Premiership Player of the Month as well as the Lumbers player of the month, voted for by Tigers supporters.

His experience helped Tigers when many of the old guard were away with England for the autumn internationals.

Josh was key in his team's 20-15 win over league leaders Gloucester, with the ex-All Black scoring 10 of the 20 points.

Beziers

12

Pens: Dubois (3), Quesada

Position	No.	Player
Full Back	15	S.Bonetti
Right Wing	14	P.Escalles
Centre	13	J-M.Aue
Centre	12	J.P.Grandclaude
Left Wing	11	T.Dejardin
Fly Half	10	J.F.Dubois
Scrum Half	9	P.Mignoni (c)
Prop	1	T.Ratiadze
Hooker	2	S.Bruno
Prop	3	S.Bonorino
Lock	4	K.Ghezal
Lock	5	T.Privat
Flanker	6	M.Dieude
Flanker	7	A.Gardiner
No.8	8	F.Gommard

Replacements: G.Quesada, G.Shvelaidze, V.Nadiradze, N.Durand, J.Laharrague, J.Selva, F.Martinez

Tigers earned a vital victory in a gruelling match that saw three players sin binned.

After losing to Northampton at Welford Road the previous weekend, this crucial win on French soil was a boost for the reigning European champions, who all but guaranteed a home tie in the quarter-finals.

The first half was try-less and Beziers made the most of their opportunities at goal to lead 6-3 going into the break.

> "Beziers are a good side – not many teams walk away from here with a victory." – **Dean Richards**

Geordan Murphy, who had taken over kicking duties from Tim Stimpson, led the team home in the second half, setting up the only two tries of the game and adding his golden boot to seal the victory. Tigers' first try came towards the end of the half when Murphy carved through the Beziers defence before offloading to Ollie Smith, who had an easy run over the line.

24 Leicester Tigers

Tries: Smith, Lloyd **Cons:** Murphy
Pens: Murphy (3) **DGs:** Kafer

Beziers' replacement goal kicker scored a penalty before full-time, putting them within two points of Tigers. However, a 76th minute try by Leon Lloyd and a decisive last minute Kafer drop goal secured the win.

Match Stats		
Tackles	52	67
Missed Tackles	12	13
Ball Carries	56	62
Metres	348	383
Defenders Beaten	9	14
Passes	97	97
Clean Breaks	4	7
Pens / Free Kicks	9	15
Turnovers	10	8
Breakdowns Won	46	57
% Line-Outs Won	71	92
% Scrums Won	100	75

Position	No.	Player
Full Back	15	G.Murphy
Right Wing	14	L.Lloyd
Centre	13	O.Smith
Centre	12	R.Kafer
Left Wing	11	F.Tuilagi
Fly Half	10	A.Healey
Scrum Half	9	T.Tierney
Prop	1	P.Freshwater
Hooker	2	D.West
Prop	3	F.Tournaire
Lock	4	M.Johnson (c)
Lock	5	L.Deacon
Flanker	6	M.Corry
Flanker	7	J.Kronfeld
No.8	8	W.Johnson

Replacements: H.Ellis, D.Garforth, G.Rowntree, B.Kay, G Chuter

Leicester Tigers   53

Tries: Tuilagi (3), Deacon, West, Kafer, Murphy, Vesty
Cons: Murphy (5) **Pens:** Murphy

Position	No.	Player
Full Back	15	G.Murphy
Right Wing	14	L.Lloyd
Centre	13	O.Smith
Centre	12	R.Kafer
Left Wing	11	F.Tuilagi
Fly Half	10	A.Healey
Scrum Half	9	T.Tierney
Prop	1	G.Rowntree
Hooker	2	D.West
Prop	3	F.Tournaire
Lock	4	M.Johnson (c)
Lock	5	L.Deacon
Flanker	6	M.Corry
Flanker	7	W.Johnson
No.8	8	A.Balding

Replacements: S.Booth, G.Chuter, H.Ellis, D.Garforth, B.Kay, P.Short, S.Vesty

Leicester Tigers showed their class in an exciting match at a packed Welford Road.

Despite an early threat from Beziers with an attempt at a drop goal in the opening minutes, Tigers dominated the visitors and were first to score with a Geordan Murphy penalty in the first 11 minutes.

Beziers were quick to respond and levelled just five minutes later. Straight from the restart a chase and steal by Tigers' No.8 Adam Balding set up the backs for a score. A misjudged pass bounced before hitting the boot of Freddie Tuilagi who chased his own kick and grounded the ball over the line inches away from the dead ball area. Murphy converted to give Tigers an important early lead.

Just short of the 30 minute mark, Murphy found holes in the Beziers defence for a sprint up the centre of the pitch. He was tackled short of the line but a ferocious Tigers pack rucked out the Frenchmen and the ball was recycled to the wing via Dorian West, who set up Louis Deacon for a score in the corner and a conversion by Murphy.

> "The backs are starting to fire again and I was very pleased with the performance. It was a very difficult game in France last weekend but we showed that we did our homework." – **Dean Richards**

Five minutes later Tigers took a lineout just 10 metres from the Beziers line. It was taken short by skipper Martin Johnson who brought the ball down for a powerful catch and drive which was touched down by West in the corner to bring the half-time score to 22-3 to Tigers.

Tigers stayed on fire into the second half and after just six minutes text book defence by Tigers trapped the visitors in their own 22 and Tigers were able to turn over the ball. A pass out left created a two-man overlap for Tigers and a pop from Murphy to a powerful Tuilagi steaming down the wing rewarded Tigers with their first score of the half which was converted by Murphy.

Shortly after, centre Rod Kafer appeared out of the mist that had enveloped the ground and weaved

10   Beziers

Tries: Nadiradze **Cons:** Quesada
Pens: Quesada

through the defence to score under the posts for an easy conversion by Murphy.

Some great link work by the backs was showcased in a third try just 20 minutes into the half. Steve Booth checked his pace down the wing to allow Austin Healey to change his line and take the ball through the Beziers defence before popping off to replacement prop Darren Garforth who powered through the centre and passed to Murphy just short of the line. Murphy converted his own try.

In the final 10 minutes of the half Tigers upped the pace to score an impressive try. Murphy exploited holes in the Beziers defence before switching with Leon Lloyd who passed to Tuilagi on the wing. He dived over the line for his third try of the afternoon.

In the dying minutes of the game, Kafer shot through the Beziers line with support from Vesty. In a classic example of sportsmanship Kafer offloaded the ball to Vesty who scored his first try for Tigers. Murphy converted to make the final score 53-10 to Tigers, securing the team's place at the top of the Pool One table.

Position	No.	Player
Full Back	15	S.Bonetti
Right Wing	14	J.Laharague
Centre	13	J-M.Aue
Centre	12	J.P.Grandclaude
Left Wing	11	A.Dejardin
Fly Half	10	G.Quesada
Scrum Half	9	P.Mignoni (c)
Prop	1	J-F.Pedesseau
Hooker	2	J.Selua
Prop	3	S.Bonorino
Lock	4	K.Ghezal
Lock	5	V.Nadiradze
Flanker	6	R.Castel
Flanker	7	F.Martinez
No.8	8	F.Mounier

Replacements: S.Chobet, D.Swarewski, J.F.Dubois, N.Durand, F.Gommard, Y.Nyanga, M.Ciore

Match Stats		
Tackles	29	95
Missed Tackles	3	35
Ball Carries	129	37
Metres	711	245
Defenders Beaten	35	5
Passes	180	60
Clean Breaks	5	1
Pens / Free Kicks	9	15
Turnovers	16	9
Breakdowns Won	92	22
% Line-Outs Won	79	65
% Scrums Won	100	75

Leicester Tigers   36

Tries: Lloyd, Chuter, Short, Smith, Balding
Cons: Vesty (4) **Pens:** Vesty

Position	No.	Player
Full Back	15	S.Booth
Right Wing	14	O.Smith
Centre	13	L.Lloyd
Centre	12	G.Gelderbloom
Left Wing	11	F.Tuilagi
Fly Half	10	S.Vesty
Scrum Half	9	J.Hamilton
Prop	1	F.Tournaire
Hooker	2	G.Chuter
Prop	3	D.Garforth
Lock	4	P.Short
Lock	5	L.Deacon
Flanker	6	M.Corry (c)
Flanker	7	A.Balding
No.8	8	W.Johnson

Replacements: L.Abraham, M.Johnson, R.Kafer, R.Nebbett, T.Tierney, D.West, J.Holtby

National Division One side, Worcester Warriors, were outclassed by a solid Leicester Tigers outfit.

Tigers piled on the pressure in the opening minutes to produce a score just eight minutes into the game. After clearing the ball from their own 22 into the Worcester half, a fumbled catch by a Worcester wing spilled the ball in front of Leon Lloyd who chipped it along the line and touched it down in the corner for the opening score.

Tigers dominated the half and despite a solid display of rugby by Worcester centre, Ben Hinshelwood, the visitors only entered the Tigers' half courtesy of penalties conceded by the home team.

> "I don't think the gulf between the leagues is that wide – Worcester caused us problems." – **Dean Richards**

Twenty-six minutes in, a typical catch and drive off a lineout gave Tigers hooker, George Chuter, a score that was converted by Sam Vesty.

Worcester livened up in the last 10 minutes and looked like they might be in for a try. However, Tigers' defence was exemplary and a tap tackle by winger John Holtby on ex-Tigers player Nnamdi Ezulike stopped the visitors from scoring.

The Warriors were persistent and some clever recycling almost rewarded them with points, but a crucial tackle by Martin Johnson stopped the attack short of the line.

Tigers kept Worcester out for the rest of the half but poor discipline allowed the visitors to put nine points on the board, leaving the half-time score at 12-9 to Tigers.

The home side continued to dominate play in the second half and were camped out in Worcester's 22 within the first five minutes with a penalty putting more points on the board.

9 Worcester Warriors

Pens: Walsh (3)

Just 11 minutes in a long misspass from Vesty and a good take by Ollie Smith fed Steve Booth the ball but he was tackled into touch short of the line. Tigers stole the resulting lineout and another catch and drive allowed Powergen man of the match, Peter Short, to score with Vesty converting.

Peter Short set up Tigers' next try with a strong run up the middle of the pitch. The ball was recycled wide and a well-angled run and dummy by full back Booth bought Tigers space to pop off to Smith in support who touched down in the corner. Vesty converted the try with a Tim Stimpson special that bounced off the posts.

Soon after, replacement scrum half Tom Tierney gave good ball to Smith who dodged past the Worcester defence to secure territory deep in the opposition 22. Another lineout set Tigers up for their third pushover try of the afternoon, this time courtesy of Adam Balding.

Despite a strong two-minute attack on Tigers' line in the dying minutes of the game, Worcester were unable to break the solid home defence, leaving the final score at 36-9 to Tigers.

Position	No.	Player
Full Back	15	H.Southwell
Right Wing	14	N.Ezulike
Centre	13	J.Ogilvie-Bull
Centre	12	B.Hinshelwood
Left Wing	11	C.Garrard
Fly Half	10	T.Walsh
Scrum Half	9	W.Swanepoel (c)
Prop	1	T.Windo
Hooker	2	C.Hall
Prop	3	A.Olver
Lock	4	D.Zaltman
Lock	5	M.Morgan
Flanker	6	R.Bates
Flanker	7	R.Nias
No.8	8	J.Jenner

Replacements: C.Chalmers, T.Richardson, N.Lyman, N.Mason, J.O'Reilly, S.Pearl, G.Pfister

Match Stats	TIGERS	WORCESTER RUGBY
Tackles	99	103
Missed Tackles	21	35
Ball Carries	108	81
Metres	421	342
Defenders Beaten	35	21
Passes	9	5
Clean Breaks	5	0
Pens / Freekick	16	7
Turnovers	16	9
Breakdowns Won	99	57
% Line-Outs Won	91	70
% Scrums Won	89	12

London Wasps
26

Tries: Lewsey, Howley **Cons:** King (2)
Pens: King (3) **DGs:** King

Position	No.	Player
Full Back	15	M.van Gisbergen
Right Wing	14	J.Lewsey
Centre	13	F.Waters
Centre	12	S.Abbott
Left Wing	11	J.Rudd
Fly Half	10	A.King
Scrum Half	9	R.Howley
Prop	1	C.Dowd
Hooker	2	T.Leota
Prop	3	W.Green
Lock	4	S.Shaw
Lock	5	R.Birkett
Flanker	6	J.Worsley
Flanker	7	P.Volley
No.8	8	L.Dallaglio (c)

Replacements: M.Denney, A.Kershaw, K.Logan, M.Purdy, P.Scrivener, M.Wood, B.Gotting

Leicester Tigers suffered a disappointing result following the Christmas break with a 26–13 loss to London Wasps at Adams Park.

After picking up three wins on the spin in December, Tigers were looking good as they went into the break 10-6 up.

Tigers absorbed the pressure in the first half and their points came from a stunning Harry Ellis try supported by the boot of Tim Stimpson.

> "We need to turn it around. We have had a habit of turning it around in the second half of the season, and this is what we've got to make sure happens now."
> **– Dean Richards**

Josh Kronfeld set up Ellis with a break from his own half. The speedy number nine was in support and took a good pass from the ex-All Black to sprint 50 metres, outpacing his opposite number Rob Howley, and scoring in the right corner.

Stimpson converted and added a penalty to Alex King's two before the break to see the visitors end the half four points up.

Wasps were quick to redress the balance in the second half and King sliced a drop goal and penalty through the posts against Stimpson's solo penalty to narrow Tigers' lead to one point.

The hosts pulled out all the stops in the final quarter and ran in a pair of tries to secure the win.

The first came from Josh Lewsey who finished off a good break from

Did you know?
This game saw the debut appearance for Tigers winger John Holtby, who rates his first try for the club on May 3 against London Irish as his best rugby moment ever.

13 Leicester Tigers

Tries: Ellis **Cons:** Stimpson
Pens: Stimpson (2)

Stuart Abbott and the second was a solo effort by Howley, who dummied the defence at a ruck 15 metres out and strolled in for a try under the posts.

Match Stats	WASPS	TIGERS
Tackles	64	101
Missed Tackles	8	16
Ball Carries	88	57
Metres	462	331
Defenders Beaten	13	8
Passes	90	67
Clean Breaks	8	0
Pens / Free Kicks	17	14
Turnovers	14	13
Breakdowns Won	70	44
% Line-Outs Won	82	100
% Scrums Won	100	93

Position	No.	Player
Full Back	15	T.Stimpson
Right Wing	14	J.Holtby
Centre	13	O.Smith
Centre	12	R.Kafer
Left Wing	11	F.Tuilagi
Fly Half	10	S.Vesty
Scrum Half	9	H.Ellis
Prop	1	D.Jelley
Hooker	2	D.West
Prop	3	D.Garforth
Lock	4	M.Johnson (c)
Lock	5	B.Kay
Flanker	6	W.Johnson
Flanker	7	J.Kronfeld
No.8	8	A.Balding

Replacements: G.Chuter, L.Deacon, G.Gelderbloom, T.Tierney, F.Tournaire, N.Back, G.Raynor

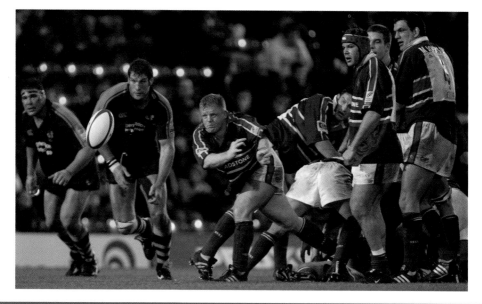

December Review

December hailed two more rounds of Heineken Cup matches and this time Tigers faced French side Beziers back to back at the start of the month. Tigers performed outstandingly in both games, beating Beziers 77-22 on aggregate and standing in good stead in Pool 1.

Tigers' next match was in round six of the Powergen Cup as they entertained division one side Worcester Warriors. Tigers beat the plucky visitors 36-9 to make it through to the quarter-finals the following month.

Tigers faced another blip in their winning streak after Christmas when they travelled to London Wasps' new home, Adams Park, ending the year with a 26-13 loss.

At the end of the year, Tigers favourite Tudor Thomas hung up his microphone as the club's matchday announcer after more than 40 years service to the club.

Snippets

Tigers players visit the LRI children's ward to hand out Christmas presents generously donated by supporters.

Tigers U21s celebrate 12 unbeaten league games in a row – putting them top of the Zurich U21s table.

Tigers Emerging beat Northampton Wanderers 15-12 in a thrilling Boxing Day match at Franklin's Gardens.

Results (Leicester Tigers' score first)

Date	Comp	Opponent	H/A	Score
Dec 8	HC	Beziers	A	24-12
Dec 14	HC	Beziers	H	53-10
Dec 21	PGC	Worcester Warriors	H	36-9
Dec 27	ZP	London Wasps	A	13-26

Key

ZP	Zurich Premiership
ZW	Zurich Wildcard
HC	Heineken Cup
PGC	Powergen Cup

ZURICH PREMIERSHIP

Team	P	W	D	L	F	A	PD	BP	Pts
Gloucester	13	10	1	2	359	213	+146	6	48
Sharks	13	8	1	4	323	296	+27	5	39
Leeds Tykes	13	7	2	4	307	262	+45	2	35
London Wasps	13	6	2	5	323	303	+20	6	34
Northampton Saints	13	7	0	6	283	226	+57	5	33
Leicester Tigers	13	7	0	6	256	235	+21	3	31
Saracens	13	6	0	7	309	354	-45	4	28
Bristol Shoguns	12	5	1	6	301	316	-15	3	25
NEC Harlequins	12	5	0	7	267	299	-32	5	25
London Irish	13	4	1	8	278	305	-27	4	22
Bath Rugby	13	4	2	7	235	297	-52	2	22
Newcastle Falcons	13	3	0	10	217	352	-135	4	16

Top Points Scorers

Name	Total
T.Stimpson	122
G.Murphy	19
H.Ellis	15
J.Kronfeld	15
N.Back	15
S.Booth	12

Top Try Scorers

Name	Total
H.Ellis	3
J.Kronfeld	3
N.Back	3
O.Smith	2
S.Booth	2
R.Kafer	2

Player Of The Month

Geordan Murphy

Geordan clocked up 29 points during December, having only recently returned from injury.

His outstanding performance against Beziers at Welford Road saw him named Heineken Man of the Match after scoring 18 points in Tigers' 53-10 thrashing of the French side.

Appearances	3
Tackles	3
Missed Tackles	1
Offloads	2
Ball Carries	23
Metres	253
Defenders Beaten	9
Clean Breaks	3
Try Passes	3
Tries Scored	1

Top Penalty Scorers

Name	Total
T.Stimpson	28
G.Murphy	3
S.Vesty	1

Top Drop Goal Scorers

Name	Total
G.Murphy	1
T.Stimpson	1
A.Healey	1

Regular season matches only

Leicester Tigers   23

Tries: Kronfeld, Lloyd, Smith
Cons: Murphy **Pens:** Murphy (2)

Position	No.	Player
Full Back	15	G.Murphy
Right Wing	14	J.Holtby
Centre	13	O.Smith
Centre	12	R.Kafer
Left Wing	11	L.Lloyd
Fly Half	10	S.Vesty
Scrum Half	9	J.Hamilton
Prop	1	D.Jelley
Hooker	2	G.Chuter
Prop	3	F.Tournaire
Lock	4	M.Johnson (c)
Lock	5	L.Deacon
Flanker	6	M.Corry
Flanker	7	J.Kronfeld
No.8	8	A.Balding

Replacements: S.Booth, D.Garforth, B.Kay, C.McMullen, T.Tierney, D.West, N.Back

A capacity crowd witnessed a narrow victory for Leicester Tigers over Saracens at an icy Welford Road.

Tigers were brilliant at times in a tense match but the combination of a slippery surface and a number of poorly judged passes resulted in several unforced errors by the home side.

Saracens capitalised on some poor handling by Tigers full back Geordan Murphy on the 10 minute mark with full back Adryan Winnan beating Jamie Hamilton over the line to touch down for the first points of the game.

> "I never felt we were going to lose – even going into half-time at 11-8 down I didn't feel unduly worried." – **Dean Richards**

With 20 minutes gone, Tigers made a break out of their own 22 initiated by Murphy and Leon Lloyd on the right of the pitch. The ball spun left via Sam Vesty and into the hands of winger John Holtby who stormed through three defenders before being tackled into touch. The resulting line-out was stolen by Tigers, setting them up for a catch and drive over the line and touch-down by Josh Kronfeld.

Both sides shared possession for the rest of the half and despite a number of attacking runs by Holtby and Murphy, Tigers were unable to take the lead.

Poor Tigers discipline let the home side down towards the end of the half and they gave away two easy penalties that were converted by Saracens fullback Adryan Winnan.

Tigers redeemed themselves with three points before half-time to close the gap, but despite bombarding the Saracens defence in a late effort to take the lead at the break, Tigers failed to make a further score, leaving the half-time score at 8-11 to Saracens.

18   Saracens

Tries: Winnan, Horan **Cons:** Goode
Pens: Winnan (2)

Tigers piled on the pressure from the kick off but despite a run of penalties awarded in their own half they were unable to secure a position in Saracens' 22. It was 15 minutes into the half before the home team levelled the score with a Murphy penalty.

Just seven minutes later a fantastic display of teamwork by Tigers and safe hands by Ollie Smith set the young centre up to dive over in the corner for Tigers' second try of the game.

A 22 drop out went horribly wrong for Saracens at the 30 minute mark and a backwards kick fell into the hands of Ben Kay who set up the first line of attack. The ball was passed out to Vesty who committed the defence down the centre of the pitch, before Smith offloaded to Lloyd who stormed over the line to extend Tigers' lead. The try was converted by Geordan Murphy to take the score to 23-11 to Tigers.

In the final minute of the game, Saracens narrowed the deficit when a charge down from a Vesty kick shuttled the ball back over Tigers' line.

Tim Horan turned on the pace to beat the Tigers defence over the line and a conversion by ex-Leicester player Andy Goode brought the final score to 23-18 to Tigers.

Position	No.	Player
Full Back	15	A.Winnan
Right Wing	14	B.Sparg
Centre	13	K.Sorrell
Centre	12	T.Shanklin
Left Wing	11	D.O'Mahony
Fly Half	10	T.Horan
Scrum Half	9	K.Bracken (c)
Prop	1	C.Califano
Hooker	2	J.Ross
Prop	3	J.Marsters
Lock	4	C.Yandell
Lock	5	S.Hooper
Flanker	6	A.Benazzi
Flanker	7	R.Hill
No.8	8	K.Chesney

Replacements: M.Cairns, R.Haughten, D.Kirton, J.Parkes, R.Peacey, M.Storey, A.Goode

Match Stats	TIGERS	SARACENS
Tackles	82	144
Missed Tackles	12	17
Ball Carries	135	65
Metres	536	282
Defenders Beaten	12	8
Passes	165	108
Clean Breaks	7	0
Penalties Conceded	12	12
Turnovers Conceded	14	12
Breakdowns Won	107	49
% Line-Outs Won	88	82
% Scrums Won	100	100

Amatori & Calvisano 22

Tries: Vaccari (3) **Cons:** Fraser (2)
Pens: Fraser

Position	No.	Player
Full Back	15	M.Ravazzolo
Right Wing	14	F.Merli
Centre	13	G.Raineri
Centre	12	C.Zanoletti
Left Wing	11	E.Muliero
Fly Half	10	G.Fraser
Scrum Half	9	J.Dragotto
Prop	1	G.Bocca
Hooker	2	A.Moretti
Prop	3	M.Castrogiovanni
Lock	4	L.Mastrodomenico
Lock	5	J.Purll
Flanker	6	A.De Rossi (c)
Flanker	7	C.Mayerhofler
No.8	8	C.Roux

Replacements: G.De Carli, S.Perugini, P.Vaccari, P.Griffin

Heineken Cup holders Leicester Tigers continued their smooth progress in this season's competition after fighting off a spirited comeback from a plucky Calvisano outfit.

Tigers opened their account after just two minutes with a soft try for quick-witted hooker George Chuter who pounced on a tapdown over the try line from a Calvisano line-out. Tim Stimpson added the conversion but missed a simple chance in front of the posts eight minutes later when scrum half Harry Ellis started and finished a fine counter-attack involving Josh Kronfeld and Martin Corry.

> "I thought they came back very strongly but we were always mindful that could happen. You've got to take your hat off to them – they never gave up and a couple of their scores were very good indeed."
> **– Dean Richards**

Kiwi fly half Gerard Fraser finally got the home side on the scoreboard with a penalty after a rare foray into the Tigers half. Steve Booth extended the Tigers lead almost immediately when Rod Kafer, playing at fly half in place of the injured Austin Healey, put in a clever diagonal kick which Geordan Murphy took on the full and off loaded to the former Rugby League winger. Leicester looked to be cruising when Stimpson powered over from eight metres and converted on the half-hour and second row Luca Mastrodomenico was sent to the sin-bin for handling in a ruck.

The Italians made a rash of substitutions at half-time and the introduction of experienced international winger Paolo Vaccari was the major factor in their impressive comeback after the restart. Despite an early try from

40 Leicester Tigers

Tries: Ellis (2), Chuter, Booth, Stimpson, Tournaire
Cons: Stimpson (5)

Ellis, the winger touched down twice during a period of 19 unanswered points which also saw number seven Chean Roux cross under the Tigers' posts.

Calvisano showed how they turned over Neath on this ground in round three of the competition and they competed exceptionally well at the break down before releasing their rejuvenated back line.

Tigers cause wasn't helped when impressive scrum half Ellis received a yellow card on the hour for a blatant shoulder charge. Tigers Director of Rugby Dean Richards was forced into bringing on Martin Johnson in an attempt to steady the ship with 10 minutes remaining. Fellow replacement Franck Tournaire was on hand to drive over following a Johnson line-out take with two minutes left on the clock. Stimpson converted to make the final score 40-22 and send the 700 travelling Tigers supporters home happy.

> "Although Ben Kay got the man-of-the-match award, I felt that Harry Ellis was outstanding. He's a very physical scrum half who's young and enthusiastic and he caused them a lot of problems."
> **– Dean Richards**

Position	No.	Player
Full Back	15	G.Murphy
Right Wing	14	T.Stimpson
Centre	13	G.Gelderbloom
Centre	12	O.Smith
Left Wing	11	S.Booth
Fly Half	10	R.Kafer
Scrum Half	9	H.Ellis
Prop	1	D.Jelley
Hooker	2	G.Chuter
Prop	3	D.Garforth
Lock	4	L.Deacon
Lock	5	B.Kay
Flanker	6	J.Kronfeld
Flanker	7	N.Back (c)
No.8	8	M.Corry

Replacements: J.Hamilton, M.Johnson, G.Raynor, F.Tournaire, F.Tuilagi, D.West, A.Balding

Match Stats		
Tackles	63	72
Missed Tackles	26	5
Ball Carries	59	72
Metres	240	299
Defenders Beaten	9	20
Passes	121	93
Clean Breaks	6	5
Pens / Free Kicks	18	13
Turnovers	11	17
Breakdowns Won	53	57
% Line-Outs Won	86	76
% Scrums Won	69	86

Leicester Tigers 36

Tries: Murphy, Hamilton, Kronfeld, Kay
Cons: Stimpson (2)   **Pens:** Stimpson (4)

Position	No.	Player
Full Back	15	G.Murphy
Right Wing	14	S.Booth
Centre	13	L.Lloyd
Centre	12	R.Kafer
Left Wing	11	T.Stimpson
Fly Half	10	S.Vesty
Scrum Half	9	H.Ellis
Prop	1	D.Jelley
Hooker	2	D.West
Prop	3	F.Tournaire
Lock	4	M.Johnson (c)
Lock	5	B.Kay
Flanker	6	W.Johnson
Flanker	7	N.Back
No.8	8	A.Balding

Replacements: G.Chuter, D.Garforth, G.Gelderbloom, J.Hamilton, J.Kronfeld, L.Moody, L.Deacon

Leicester Tigers thrashed Neath 36-11 in one of their best performances of the season. The Welford Road faithful were entertained by four tries in a win that secured a home fixture for the quarter-finals of the Heineken Cup.

Tigers regained possession straight from their kick off and a series of aggressive runs tested the Neath defence. A three on two on the left wing set up Geordan Murphy to pace through the gap for an easy score in the first minute, but Stimpson missed the conversion.

Just three minutes later Stimpson redeemed himself with a penalty in front of the posts courtesy of poor gamesmanship by Neath prop Adam Jones. Tigers' Golden Boot increased the home team's lead on the eight minute mark with a second penalty.

From the restart Neath secured possession, finding space out wide to send international wing Shane Williams over the line. The visitors soon tightened the gap with a drop-goal by fly half Shaun Connor.

> "They caused us some problems. We dominated possession, but still found it hard to score tries. We managed to get across for a few at the end."
> – **Martin Johnson**

Tigers were unable to extend their lead after Stimpson missed a penalty kick, but a second chance came as Tigers opted for a line-out from a further penalty which took them to just ten metres from the Neath try line. The ball was spun to the centres and secured by Rod Kafer who charged down the middle of the pitch. Replacement scrum half Jamie Hamilton looked to recycle the ball from the back of the ruck but as a gap opened, the speedy half back danced through the Neath defence to score under the posts for an easy conversion from Stimpson. Neath continued to challenge Tigers' defence but the determined home side kept them at bay.

The visitors looked dangerous from the start of the second half, stealing the ball from the kick off and keeping Tigers out of their half for the first two

11   Neath

minutes. However, Tigers capitalised on a stolen ball at a Neath line-out and Sam Vesty spun the ball wide to Leon Lloyd who made good ground before being tackled. The resulting ruck awarded Tigers a penalty, allowing Stimpson to take his penalty tally to four.

Tigers lost focus for a while and poor discipline awarded Neath a string of penalties, one of which made an easy three points for the visitors. The rest of the half showcased some impressive runs from Tigers players. At the 60 minute mark a Kay challenge smashed the Neath defence, but a supporting run, maul and drive over the line by Dorian West was denied a try by the referee who judged it to be held up, awarding Tigers a five metre scrum.

Tigers continued to wear down the Neath defence. A tactical replacement by Tigers to bring on international stars Josh Kronfeld and Lewis Moody paid dividends as just one minute later a drive down the right wing, powered by Kronfeld, was converted into points as he touched down over the line with Stimpson adding a further two points.

Tigers' 'dream team' back row worked more of their magic less than two minutes later and a well-timed pass to Kay saw the sturdy lock crash over the line to further the lead and leave the final score at 36-11 to Tigers.

Position	No.	Player
Full Back	15	A.Durston
Right Wing	14	G.Morris
Centre	13	J.Storey
Centre	12	D.Tiueti
Left Wing	11	S.Williams
Fly Half	10	S.Connor
Scrum Half	9	P.Horgan
Prop	1	D.Jones
Hooker	2	B.Williams
Prop	3	A.Jones
Lock	4	A.Newman
Lock	5	G.Llewellyn (c)
Flanker	6	B.Sinkinson
Flanker	7	S.Tandy
No.8	8	R.Phillips

Replacements: A.Bateman, A.Matthews, P.James, L.Jarvis, S.Martin, A.Millward, A.Mocelutu

Match Stats	LEICESTER TIGERS	
Tackles	80	139
Missed Tackles	13	29
Ball Carries	112	63
Metres	357	263
Defenders Beaten	18	15
Passes	133	96
Clean Breaks	6	1
Pens / Free Kicks	10	13
Turnovers	14	16
Breakdowns Won	98	52
% Line-Outs Won	93	77
% Scrums Won	93	100

NEC Harlequins   12

Pens: Burke (4)

Position	No.	Player
Full Back	15	N.Williams
Right Wing	14	D.Luger
Centre	13	W.Greenwood
Centre	12	V.Satala
Left Wing	11	B.Gollings
Fly Half	10	P.Burke
Scrum Half	9	S.Bemand
Prop	1	J.Leonard
Hooker	2	T.Fuga
Prop	3	J.Dawson
Lock	4	B.Davison
Lock	5	A.Codling
Flanker	6	A.Tiatia
Flanker	7	A.Vos (c)
No.8	8	T.Diprose

Replacements: P.Cardinalli, R.Jewell, S.Miall, M.Moore, M.Powell, L.Sherriff, J.Evans

Leicester Tigers turned round a three-year run of bad luck at The Stoop to beat Harlequins 19-12 and progress to the semi-finals of the Powergen Cup.

Tigers outscored the London side two tries to nil, with Paul Burke kicking the only points for the hosts.

Leicester Tigers' more colourful display saw them rewarded with two tries in the first half. It would have been three but for a controversial decision by referee Chris White which meant a stunning Jamie Hamilton score was disallowed.

Tim Stimpson crossed the line first after levelling the score at 3-3 just ten minutes in. Having set up the ball deep in the Harlequins half, skipper Martin Johnson secured the line-out ball which was recycled through Hamilton to Stimpson on the wing who dived over for the opening try.

> "We have lost a couple of cup games here but they haven't beaten us in the league for 10 years."
> – Martin Johnson

Tigers' second try came just 15 minutes later when Moody, atoning for his earlier sin binning, teamed up with Geordan Murphy to storm down the right wing and fly over in the corner, giving Tigers a 13-6 lead at the break.

Tigers benefitted from the lion's share of possession in the second half but were unable to turn pressure into points.

Both sides kicked two penalties apiece in the second half to bring the final score to 19-12 and overcome Tigers' so-called curse at The Stoop and book them a place in the semis.

19   Leicester Tigers

Tries: Stimpson, Moody
Pens: Stimpson (3)

Did you know?
Tigers had been knocked out of the cup the last three seasons at The Stoop - twice by Harlequins and once by London Irish.

Position	No.	Player
Full Back	15	T.Stimpson
Right Wing	14	G.Murphy
Centre	13	O.Smith
Centre	12	R.Kafer
Left Wing	11	L.Lloyd
Fly Half	10	S.Vesty
Scrum Half	9	J.Hamilton
Prop	1	G.Rowntree
Hooker	2	D.West
Prop	3	F.Tournaire
Lock	4	M.Johnson (c)
Lock	5	B.Kay
Flanker	6	L.Moody
Flanker	7	J.Kronfeld
No.8	8	M.Corry

Replacements: P.Freshwater, N.Back, A.Balding, S.Booth, G.Chuter, D.Garforth, T.Tierney

Match Stats	NEC HARLEQUINS	LEICESTER TIGERS
Tackles	96	78
Missed Tackles	16	14
Ball Carries	63	82
Metres	120	304
Defenders Beaten	14	13
Passes	107	113
Clean Breaks	1	2
Pens / Free Kicks	9	15
Turnovers	8	15
Breakdowns Won	54	70
% Line-Outs Won	90	92
% Scrums Won	82	100

January Review

Tigers turned over a new leaf in the New Year, winning all of their January matches. For the second month in a row, it was a bag of allsorts fixture-wise with two Heineken Cup matches, a Premiership fixture and the Powergen Cup quarter-final.

The team and over 1,000 supporters travelled to Italy on January 11 for the second leg of the Amatori & Calvisano fixture. This awesome level of support, with almost half of the crowd made up of Tigers fans, certainly boosted the side who went on to beat the Italians 40-22.

A convincing 36-11 win over Neath the following week secured Tigers' position at the top of the Pool 1 table and a home fixture for the quarter-finals.

The last game of the month proved third time lucky for Tigers, who were drawn against Harlequins in the Powergen Cup for the third consecutive season. This time Tigers pulled it out of the bag to win 19-12 and face Gloucester in March at Franklin's Gardens, Northampton.

Snippets

Welford and Graham Rowntree went along to a scrummaging session at The Shires shopping centre in Leicester to promote front row safety and help recruit new players for local clubs.

Tigers' Heineken Cup match against Neath is the first ever pool match to be sold out at Welford Road. The 16,845 capacity also makes it the largest crowd for a European pool game in Great Britain and Ireland.

Results (Leicester Tigers' score first)

Jan 4	ZP	Saracens	H	23-18
Jan 11	HC	Amatori & Calvisano	A	40-22
Jan 18	HC	Neath	H	36-11
Jan 25	PGC	NEC Harlequins	A	19-12

Key

ZP	Zurich Premiership
ZW	Zurich Wildcard
HC	Heineken Cup
PGC	Powergen Cup

Team	P	W	D	L	F	A	PD	BP	Pts
Gloucester	14	11	1	2	383	230	+153	6	52
Sharks	14	9	1	4	361	299	+62	6	44
Leeds Tykes	14	8	2	4	327	269	+58	3	39
Leicester Tigers	14	8	0	6	279	253	+26	3	35
London Wasps	14	6	2	6	340	327	+13	7	35
Northampton Saints	14	7	0	7	293	248	+45	5	33
NEC Harlequins	13	6	0	7	293	316	-23	5	29
Saracens	14	6	0	8	327	377	-50	5	29
London Irish	14	5	1	8	300	315	-15	4	26
Bristol Shoguns	13	5	1	7	318	342	-24	3	25
Bath Rugby	14	4	2	8	242	317	-75	2	22
Newcastle Falcons	14	3	0	11	220	390	-170	4	16

Top Points Scorers

Name	Total
T.Stimpson	122
G.Murphy	27
J.Kronfeld	20
O.Smith	15
H.Ellis	15
N.Back	15

Top Try Scorers

Name	Total
J.Kronfeld	4
O.Smith	3
H.Ellis	3
N.Back	3
L.Lloyd	2
S.Booth	2

Top Penalty Scorers

Name	Total
T.Stimpson	28
G.Murphy	5
S.Vesty	1

Player Of The Month

Harry Ellis

Appearances	2
Tackles	4
Missed Tackles	0
Ball Carries	9
Metres	75
Passes	61
Defenders Beaten	5
Tries Scored	2
Average Gain Per Carry	5.5m

Harry was named player of the month after sterling performances in the Heineken Cup, notably at Calvisano where he scored two great tries.

Harry is a prime example of Tigers' strength in depth, having made his way through the ranks from the academy to the first team squad.

Top Drop Goal Scorers

Name	Total
G.Murphy	1
T.Stimpson	1
A.Healey	1

Regular season matches only

Bath Rugby   8

Tries: Danielli
Pens: Barkley

Position	No.	Player
Full Back	15	M.Perry
Right Wing	14	S.Danielli
Centre	13	K.Maggs
Centre	12	S.Davy
Left Wing	11	O.Barkley
Fly Half	10	M.Catt
Scrum Half	9	G.Cooper
Prop	1	D.Barnes
Hooker	2	J.Humphreys
Prop	3	J.Mallett
Lock	4	S.Borthwick
Lock	5	D.Grewcock (c)
Flanker	6	A.Beattie
Flanker	7	A.Vander
No.8	8	N.Thomas

Replacements: A.Crockett, S.Emms, A.Galasso, L.Mears, G.Thomas, T.Voyce, A.Williams

Leicester Tigers shot into the Premiership top three in a troubled game against Bath at The Rec, beating the West country side 15-8.

Tigers didn't win the game as much as Bath lost it, but it was the Leicester resilience that shone through to take the victory.

Bath took the lead early on with an Olly Barkley penalty in the first ten minutes. The hosts increased the gap with the opening try of the game, courtesy of Scotland wing Simon Danielli.

> "I think last season, and the three seasons prior to that, we made a habit of sometimes playing badly and coming out with the points, and that's what happened today." – **Dean Richards**

The try came as Tigers made a bid to escape the Bath 22. Geordan Murphy looked to kick then opted for the pass to winger Leon Lloyd, whose sloppy offload fell into the hands of Danielli, who made the most of the error and shot over the line.

15 Leicester Tigers

Tries: Kay, Murphy **Cons:** Murphy
Pens: Vesty

Tigers were quick to make up for their error and lock Ben Kay, in almost mirror fashion to Bath's earlier try, intercepted the ball to charge in the visitors' first five points just two minutes later. Murphy added the extras, narrowing the gap to a solitary point as the teams went in for the break.

The second half was much the same, with numerous handling errors putting both teams in danger, but it was Tigers who benefitted and fly half Sam Vesty brought in three points to take the lead, before Murphy extended it by five with a try in the 71st minute.

Tigers held out despite a late attack by Bath to leave the final score at 15-8.

> "I agree with (Bath coach) Michael Foley that the execution and the skill levels were not high but, if you look back, how many times in Leicester-Bath games has that not been the case? I'd say on very few occasions." — **Dean Richards**

Position	No.	Player
Full Back	15	G.Murphy
Right Wing	14	L.Lloyd
Centre	13	O.Smith
Centre	12	R.Kafer
Left Wing	11	F.Tuilagi
Fly Half	10	S.Vesty
Scrum Half	9	J.Hamilton
Prop	1	G.Rowntree
Hooker	2	D.West
Prop	3	D.Garforth
Lock	4	M.Johnson (c)
Lock	5	B.Kay
Flanker	6	L.Moody
Flanker	7	N.Back
No.8	8	M.Corry

Replacements: G.Chuter, G.Gelderbloom, J.Kronfeld, T.Tierney, A.Balding, S.Booth, F.Tournaire

Match Stats		
Tackles	46	71
Missed Tackles	10	14
Ball Carries	63	49
Metres	300	393
Defenders Beaten	15	10
Passes	121	82
Clean Breaks	1	0
Pens / Free Kicks	13	11
Turnovers	11	7
Breakdowns Won	44	27
% Line-Outs Won	88	98
% Scrums Won	100	100

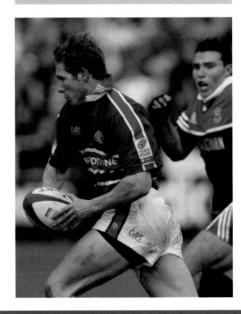

Leicester Tigers 40

Tries: Murphy (2), Kronfeld, Smith, Kafer, Booth
Cons: Murphy (2), Stimpson (3)

Position	No.	Player
Full Back	15	G.Murphy
Right Wing	14	L.Lloyd
Centre	13	O.Smith
Centre	12	R.Kafer
Left Wing	11	F.Tuilagi
Fly Half	10	S.Vesty
Scrum Half	9	J.Hamilton
Prop	1	G.Rowntree
Hooker	2	D.West
Prop	3	F.Tournaire
Lock	4	M.Johnson (c)
Lock	5	L.Deacon
Flanker	6	L.Moody
Flanker	7	J.Kronfeld
No.8	8	M.Corry

Replacements: G.Chuter, D.Garforth, T.Stimpson, T.Tierney, N.Back, A.Balding, S.Booth

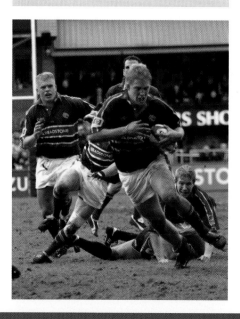

Leicester Tigers moved to third place in the Premiership after a crushing victory over Bristol.

The visitors started well and within the first minute had regained the ball from the kick off. They put Tigers under pressure and looked like they might get an early score. However, a well-drilled defence and a set of crunching tackles by Freddie Tuilagi kept Bristol at bay.

Tigers fought back and work by Lewis Moody and Ollie Smith put them well into the Bristol half. On the eight minute mark, Martin Corry made yards through the centre of the pitch before the ball was spun out to Sam Vesty, who off-loaded to Smith and on to Geordan Murphy who paced over the line and touched the ball down under the posts. Murphy converted his own try.

The half continued with both teams unable to get over the line. Some good forward drives and back play by the home team was halted by a solid Bristol defence.

> "A performance like this was always going to happen at this stage. It's taken us a while to get the confidence to play like that." – **Dean Richards**

It wasn't until the last minutes of the half that Vesty found a gap in the defence and off-loaded to Rod Kafer. He spun out to Leon Lloyd before the ball found Murphy, who weaved through the defence to score his second try of the match to the right of the posts. Murphy converted.

After missing his two earlier penalties, Felipe Contepomi notched up two in injury time to leave the half time score at 14-6 to Tigers.

Tigers started the second half and both teams were keen to impress. Just under 10 minutes in, Tigers put pressure on Bristol's left wing and Josh Kronfeld popped out of a driving maul to score in the corner.

Tigers played some excellent attacking rugby in the half but handling errors mixed with controversial refereeing decisions held the team back.

Powerful drives by Moody and Kronfeld gained Tigers yards but the home team were unable to finish

6   **Bristol Shoguns**

Pens: Contepomi (2)

despite impressive sprints up the wing by Lloyd.

It wasn't until the last ten minutes that Tigers put valuable points on the board. Tigers built forward momentum and the ball found Smith in the centre. Neil Back was in support and fixed his opposite man to make a space for Smith, who charged through to score under the posts. Tim Stimpson converted.

Just two minutes later, Tigers picked up a vital bonus point following a forward drive by Adam Balding. Vesty picked up and made ground, offloading to Kafer who strolled unopposed over the Bristol line to ground the ball under the posts. Stimpson converted.

Tigers looked like they they would score another when Back made yards and offloaded to Smith. Smith popped a sneaky backhand pass for Murphy and would have pulled it off but for an unfortunate knock on.

Tigers were still on the hunt for points in the dying minutes of the game and were rewarded after a Vesty interception. Vesty set the defence and offloaded to Steve Booth, who passed five defenders to scamper a try in under the posts. A conversion by Stimpson brought the final score to 40-6 to Tigers.

Position	No.	Player
Full Back	15	J.Williams
Right Wing	14	D.Rees
Centre	13	M.Shaw
Centre	12	D.Gibson (c)
Left Wing	11	P.Christophers
Fly Half	10	F.Contepomi
Scrum Half	9	A.Pichot
Prop	1	A.Sheridan
Hooker	2	P.Johnstone
Prop	3	D.Crompton
Lock	4	S.Morgan
Lock	5	A.Brown
Flanker	6	M.Salter
Flanker	7	M.Lipman
No.8	8	R.Beattie

Replacements: E.Bergamaschi, L.Best, S.Drahm, C.Morgan, S.Nelson, R.Oakley, P.Richards

Match Stats	LEICESTER TIGERS	BRISTOL SHOGUNS
Tackles	81	92
Missed Tackles	19	19
Ball Carries	85	75
Metres	397	353
Defenders Beaten	20	22
Passes	116	119
Clean Breaks	10	4
Penalties Conceded	15	10
Turnovers Conceded	12	16
Breakdowns Won	68	62
% Line-Outs Won	77	69
% Scrums Won	100	81

February Review

With the Six Nations afoot, February was a relatively quiet, but successful, month for Tigers. Two Premiership matches were packed into the first eight days with Tigers beating Bath 15-8 and Bristol Shoguns 40-6.

The Bristol match was Darren Garforth's 200th Premiership appearance for Leicester Tigers. The stalwart prop is the first ever player in the English Premiership to reach the landmark which has taken him since September 1991 when he made his debut for the club at the age of 25.

Later in the month, Tigers were named Team of the Year at the Leicester Mercury Sports Awards in a ceremony at De Montfort Hall. Tigers Director of Rugby, Dean Richards, was also runner-up in the coach/manager category.

Snippets

An incredible 20 Tigers players were named in England squads to take on France in the Six Nations, from England U19s to the senior side.

Darren Garforth and Perry Freshwater entertained a packed Tiger Bar at the February members evening where Darren confirmed he would retire at the end of the season.

Results

Feb 1	ZP	Bath Rugby	A	15-8
Feb 8	ZP	Bristol Shoguns	H	40-6

Key

ZP	Zurich Premiership
ZW	Zurich Wildcard
HC	Heineken Cup
PGC	Powergen Cup

ZURICH PREMIERSHIP

Team	P	W	D	L	F	A	PD	BP	Pts
Gloucester	16	13	1	2	441	268	+173	6	60
Sharks	16	11	1	4	429	310	+119	7	53
Leicester Tigers	16	10	0	6	334	267	+67	4	44
Leeds Tykes	16	9	2	5	356	298	+58	4	44
London Wasps	16	8	2	6	391	347	+44	8	44
Northampton Saints	16	8	0	8	336	289	+47	7	39
Saracens	16	6	0	10	374	440	-66	6	30
NEC Harlequins	15	6	0	9	310	393	-83	5	29
London Irish	16	5	1	10	322	373	-51	4	26
Bristol Shoguns	15	5	1	9	336	399	-63	4	26
Newcastle Falcons	16	5	0	11	269	419	-150	5	25
Bath Rugby	16	4	2	10	266	361	-95	3	23

Top Points Scorers

Name	Total
T.Stimpson	128
G.Murphy	48
J.Kronfeld	25
O.Smith	20
S.Booth	17
R.Kafer	15

Top Try Scorers

Name	Total
J.Kronfeld	5
G.Murphy	4
O.Smith	4
S.Booth	3
R.Kafer	3
H.Ellis	3

Top Penalty Scorers

Name	Total
T.Stimpson	28
G.Murphy	5
S.Vesty	2

Top Drop Goal Scorers

Name	Total
G.Murphy	1
T.Stimpson	1
A.Healey	1

Regular season matches only

Player Of The Month

Martin Johnson

As well as captaining Tigers in February, Martin Johnson's England side won both Six Nations opening games, beating France and Wales, and he later led England to the Grand Slam.

Appearances	2
Tackles	7
Missed Tackles	2
Ball Carries	6
Metres	26
Turnover Won	0
Defenders Beaten	0
Clean Breaks	1
Total Lineouts	9
Tries Scored	0

Leicester Tigers   1 1

Tries: Kronfeld
Pens: Stimpson (2)

Position	No.	Player
Full Back	15	T.Stimpson
Right Wing	14	G.Murphy
Centre	13	O.Smith
Centre	12	R.Kafer
Left Wing	11	L.Lloyd
Fly Half	10	S.Vesty
Scrum Half	9	J.Hamilton
Prop	1	G.Rowntree
Hooker	2	D.West
Prop	3	D.Garforth
Lock	4	M.Johnson (c)
Lock	5	B.Kay
Flanker	6	M.Corry
Flanker	7	J.Kronfeld
No.8	8	A.Balding

Replacements: S.Booth, P.Freshwater, W.Johnson, W.Skinner, T.Tierney, F.Tuilagi, G.Chuter

Leicester Tigers visited Franklin's Gardens for the second time this season, but the match could not have been more different to Tigers' performance just four months earlier, when they turned in a sterling performance to beat Saints 16-3.

Despite being first to score with a Tim Stimpson penalty after three minutes, Tigers failed to perform in the first half and rarely threatened the Gloucester line.

Gloucester turned down a series of kickable penalties in favour of territory which kept their points down, until Tigers flanker Josh Kronfeld gave away an easy penalty for Ludovic Mercier to slot through the posts and level the scores.

> "We didn't play well on the day and we didn't deserve to win."– **Dean Richards**

Stimpson kicked Tigers into the lead in first half injury time as his team went into the break 6-3 up.

Both teams battled for territory after half-time but neither could break through the solid walls of defence. The 55th minute saw a weakness as Gloucester wing Marcel Garvey was well placed to support full back Thinus Delport and take the ball over the line.

Gloucester must have hit a Tigers weak spot and just minutes later Thinus Delport stormed through the defence to score a try of his own, extending the cherry & whites' lead. Mercier failed to convert for the second time, leaving Gloucester's lead at seven points.

The teams continued to test each other but it was Tigers' turn for a try when Kronfeld charged over to put his team in with a chance of drawing level. The score came from a typical

16 Gloucester

Tries: Delport, Garvey
Pens: Mercier (2)

Leicester maul and gave the side the boost they needed to push for the win, two points down after Stimpson missed the goal.

Mercier picked up three points just two minutes from time to leave Tigers in need of six points to win. The men in green really pressurised the Gloucester line and as the clock wore down they camped in the opposition 22.

A series of scrums were awarded and Tigers were left at a disadvantage when Gloucester prop Rodrigo Roncero went off and the referee ordered the scrums go uncontested.

Tigers pushed for the try they desperately needed but Gloucester held out. A turnover seconds from the end took Tigers' hopes away and bought the West Country side their tickets to the final.

Position	No.	Player
Full Back	15	T.Delport
Right Wing	14	M.Garvey
Centre	13	J.Simpson-Daniel
Centre	12	H.Paul
Left Wing	11	T.Beim
Fly Half	10	L.Mercier
Scrum Half	9	A.Gomersall
Prop	1	R.Roncero
Hooker	2	O.Azam
Prop	3	A.Deacon
Lock	4	R.Fidler
Lock	5	M.Cornwell
Flanker	6	J.Boer (c)
Flanker	7	A.Hazell
No.8	8	J.Forrester

Replacements: C.Stuart-Smith, S.Amor, C.Catling, J.Paramore, T.Woodman, A.Eustace, C.Fortey

Did you know?
Leicester Tigers' first cup final at Twickenham was against Gloucester on April 15, 1978. On this occasion Gloucester won 6-3 with the penalty goal for Tigers being scored by Dusty Hare.

Match Stats	TIGERS	GLOUCESTER RFC
Tackles	53	117
Missed Tackles	21	11
Ball Carries	86	53
Metres	318	280
Defenders Beaten	14	24
Passes	106	104
Clean Breaks	2	5
Pens / Free Kicks	11	19
Turnovers	15	14
Breakdowns Won	76	40
% Line-Outs Won	85	75
% Scrums Won	100	82

Newcastle Falcons 24

Tries: Stephenson, Noon **Cons:** Wilkinson
Pens: Wilkinson (3) **DGs:** Wilkinson

Position	No.	Player
Full Back	15	J.Shaw
Right Wing	14	T.May
Centre	13	J.Noon
Centre	12	M.Mayerhofler
Left Wing	11	M.Stephenson
Fly Half	10	J.Wilkinson (c)
Scrum Half	9	J.Grindal
Prop	1	I.Peel
Hooker	2	N.Makin
Prop	3	M.Hurter
Lock	4	M.Andrews
Lock	5	S.Grimes
Flanker	6	E.Taione
Flanker	7	A.Mower
No.8	8	H.Vyvyan

Replacements: H.Charlton, P.Dowson, P.Godman, M.Thompson, C.Hamilton, G.Maclure, M.Ward

Newcastle Falcons held on against Tigers, surviving an agonising final 10 minutes with only 13 players to hold on for a tense 24-22 victory.

With key forwards Mark Andrews and Andrew Mower in the sin-bin after incurring the wrath of referee Tony Spreadbury, the home side were left with a major uphill struggle to lift themselves off the bottom of the table and ease the relegation pressure, but despite conceding two tries in that period they managed just that.

Two men to the good and with momentum swinging their way, Leicester looked to be on course for the points when Dorian West rumbled over from a catch-and-drive at an attacking line-out in the 72nd minute, but the missed conversion of Australian fly half Craig McMullen was to come back and haunt him.

When Leicester repeated the feat on the stroke of 80 minutes, West again being one of a host of forwards who appeared to have hands on the ball at the crucial scoring point, a well-taken conversion from full back Steve Booth – in for Geordan Murphy – got them to within two points.

Time was not on their side though and the Tigers were left with a lot of work to do in order to realise their top-three play-off ambitions, while Newcastle were left with slightly less relegation pressure hanging over them after a gritty performance.

Earlier they had surged into a 21-10 lead courtesy of tries through England cap Michael Stephenson and his fellow academy product Jamie Noon – Stephenson's score coming from a break involving back-row Hugh Vyvyan and Tongan back-row Epi Taione, who was not involved with his national side's hammering of Korea in a World Cup qualifier at the weekend.

That score came after Booth had fired Leicester into an early

22 Leicester Tigers

Tries: Booth, West [2] **Cons:** McMullen, Booth
Pens: Booth

lead on 15 minutes after joining the line from full back at a scrum and going over, McMullen converting.

> "We should have won. Some crucial decisions didn't go our way and we didn't take full advantage when they had two men off the field, although we did score one try in that period. But we should have done better." – **Dean Richards**

It was to be Noon's second half try that swung the game the way of the home side, kicking ahead on the counter attack and just getting to the ball before it bounced out after flat-footing the Tigers' defence.

A penalty from Wilkinson near the end, before the late Leicester onslaught, was to prove crucial – the good news for England coach Clive Woodward being that Wilkinson came through the entire 80 minutes without any recurrence of the shoulder injury that forced him from the field early against Italy at the weekend.

Position	No.	Player
Full Back	15	S.Booth
Right Wing	14	L.Lloyd
Centre	13	O.Smith
Centre	12	R.Kafer
Left Wing	11	F.Tuilagi
Fly Half	10	C.McMullen
Scrum Half	9	T.Tierney
Prop	1	P.Freshwater
Hooker	2	D.West
Prop	3	F.Tournaire
Lock	4	M.Johnson [c]
Lock	5	L.Deacon
Flanker	6	M.Corry
Flanker	7	J.Kronfeld
No.8	8	A.Balding

Replacements: N.Back, G.Gelderbloom, J.Hamilton, B.Kay, G.Rowntree, S.Vesty, D.Garforth

Match Stats	NEWCASTLE FALCONS	LEICESTER TIGERS
Tackles	138	49
Missed Tackles	22	14
Ball Carries	46	114
Metres	379	287
Defenders Beaten	9	17
Passes	80	178
Clean Breaks	4	0
Pens / Free Kicks	12	10
Turnovers	12	10
Breakdowns Won	37	106
% Line-Outs Won	83	94
% Scrums Won	100	92

March Review

As the Six Nations moved into its second month, Tigers' season took a turn for the worse. After a six-in-a-row winning streak, Tigers lost to both Gloucester in the Powergen Cup semi-final and Newcastle Falcons at Kingston Park.

The Powergen Cup result was a particular blow with Tigers losing to Gloucester by just five points after scrums went uncontested in the final 10 minutes of the game. An appeal by Tigers was not upheld and Gloucester went on to win the competition.

The highlight of the month was welcoming the Barbarians to Welford Road. As part of Neil Back's testimonial season, a Leicester XV took on a star-studded Barbarians side.

Proceeds were split between Neil and the families of two Leicestershire policemen who died on duty in 2002. The match was a great success and is set to be a regular fixture in future seasons.

Snippets

Ollie Smith made his full England debut against Italy in the Six Nations.

Hundreds of Tigers supporters pledge to return their tickets for the Heineken Cup match against Munster so the game can be played at Welford Road.

Leicester Tigers relaunch their website on www.leicestertigers.com

Results (Leicester Tigers' score first)				
Mar 1	PGC	Gloucester	A	11-16
Mar 16	ZP	Newcastle Falcons	A	22-24

Key

ZP	Zurich Premiership
ZW	Zurich Wildcard
HC	Heineken Cup
PGC	Powergen Cup

ZURICH PREMIERSHIP

Team	P	W	D	L	F	A	PD	BP	Pts
Gloucester	17	14	1	2	479	289	+190	7	65
Sharks	17	12	1	4	461	330	+131	8	58
London Wasps	18	10	2	6	446	390	+56	9	53
Leicester Tigers	17	10	0	7	356	291	+65	5	45
Leeds Tykes	17	9	2	6	376	330	+46	4	44
Northampton Saints	17	9	0	8	363	299	+64	7	43
NEC Harlequins	17	7	0	10	367	447	-80	7	35
Bristol Shoguns	17	6	1	10	405	478	-73	5	31
Saracens	18	6	0	12	414	512	-98	7	31
Newcastle Falcons	18	6	0	12	305	454	-149	6	30
Bath Rugby	18	5	2	11	306	397	-91	4	28
London Irish	17	5	1	11	328	389	-61	4	26

Top Points Scorers

Name	Total
T.Stimpson	128
G.Murphy	48
S.Booth	27
J.Kronfeld	25
O.Smith	20
D.West	15

Top Try Scorers

Name	Total
J.Kronfeld	5
S.Booth	4
G.Murphy	4
O.Smith	4
D.West	3
R.Kafer	3

Top Penalty Scorers

Name	Total
T.Stimpson	28
G.Murphy	5
S.Vesty	2
S.Booth	1

Top Drop Goal Scorers

Name	Total
G.Murphy	1
T.Stimpson	1
A.Healey	1

Regular season matches only

Player Of The Month

Josh Kronfeld

A firm favourite with the supporters, Josh picked up the award for a second time this season.

The ex-All Black was involved in both of Tigers' February games and scored a try against Gloucester in the Powergen Cup semi-final at Northampton.

Appearances	2
Tackles	13
Missed Tackles	3
Ball Carries	24
Metres	82
Defenders Beaten	2
Clean Breaks	2
Tries Scored	1

Leicester Tigers 33

Tries: Healey, Murphy, Lloyd, Tuilagi
Cons: Stimpson (2) **Pens:** Stimpson (3)

Position	No.	Player
Full Back	15	T.Stimpson
Right Wing	14	G.Murphy
Centre	13	L.Lloyd
Centre	12	F.Tuilagi
Left Wing	11	S.Booth
Fly Half	10	A.Healey
Scrum Half	9	T.Tierney
Prop	1	P.Freshwater
Hooker	2	D.West
Prop	3	D.Garforth
Lock	4	M.Johnson (c)
Lock	5	M.Corry
Flanker	6	J.Kronfeld
Flanker	7	N.Back
No.8	8	W.Johnson

Replacements: A.Balding, G.Chuter, G.Gelderbloom, G.Raynor, F.Tournaire, S.Vesty, B.Kay

Leicester Tigers boss Dean Richards praised skipper Martin Johnson as an "example to others throughout his career" as his side thumped second placed Sale 33-20 in a niggly match at Welford Road.

The tone was set with a series of bust-ups in an ill-tempered opening quarter. Referee Steve Lander regained some control when Sharks flanker Peter Anglesea was sent to the bin for dangerous use of the boot after 15 minutes.

Tigers maverick Austin Healey marked his return to first team action with the opening try after an electric break down the right from Irish winger Geordan Murphy. He pulled the defence out wide before an inside pop to Healey, who scrambled over the line to open the scoring for Tigers.

Murphy then added a try of his own from 20 metres after Healey returned the favour and worked the ball into the Sale 22 with outside centre Leon Lloyd. Lloyd travelled down the right wing and offloaded to Murphy who scored in the corner.

Stimpson converted and then added two more penalties to the Tigers' tally, with Lloyd turning on

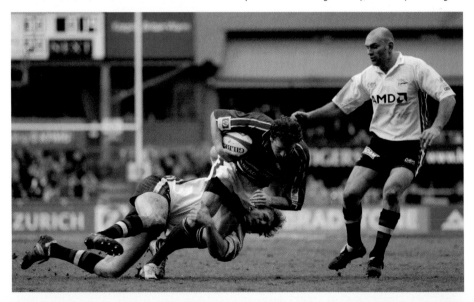

20

Sharks

Tries: Bond, Schofield **Cons:** Baxendell (2)
Pens: Baxendell (2)

the pace to break through the Sale defence and score a try of his own, converted by Stimpson with the home side looking strong two minutes from the break leading 25-0.

> "It was vitally important for us to get five points today if we are to challenge for the top three. I would agree that it was a full-blooded encounter but that's nothing unusual. Leicester-Sale matches have always been a bit like that over the years." – **Dean Richards**

Tigers then fell asleep and allowed Sale to pull back to 25-14 in two minutes courtesy of tries by centre Graeme Bond and second row Dean Schofield. Makeshift fly half Joss Baxendell converted both and added two penalties after the break but was unable to put the visitors on top.

An early try in the second half from inside centre Freddie Tuilagi secured a bonus point for the home team and a late Stimpson penalty increased the home side's lead to leave the final score at 33-20 to Tigers.

Position	No.	Player
Full Back	15	J.Robinson
Right Wing	14	M.Cueto
Centre	13	D.Harris
Centre	12	G.Bond
Left Wing	11	S.Hanley
Fly Half	10	J.Baxendell
Scrum Half	9	B.Redpath (c)
Prop	1	K.Yates
Hooker	2	A.Titterell
Prop	3	S.Turner
Lock	4	C.Jones
Lock	5	D.Schofield
Flanker	6	P.Davies
Flanker	7	S.Pinkerton
No.8	8	P.Anglesea

Replacements: A.Elliott, I.Fullerton, V.Going, C.Marais, J.Thorp, N.Walshe, R.Wilks

Match Stats		
Tackles	95	110
Missed Tackles	23	14
Ball Carries	98	91
Metres	296	353
Defenders Beaten	16	24
Passes	145	112
Clean Breaks	5	0
Pens / Free Kicks	15	15
Turnovers	10	11
Breakdowns Won	86	73
% Line-Outs Won	94	96
% Scrums Won	100	100

Leicester Tigers 7

Tries: Booth
Cons: Stimpson

Position	No.	Player
Full Back	15	T.Stimpson
Right Wing	14	G.Murphy
Centre	13	L.Lloyd
Centre	12	F.Tuilagi
Left Wing	11	S.Booth
Fly Half	10	A.Healey
Scrum Half	9	T.Tierney
Prop	1	P.Freshwater
Hooker	2	D.West
Prop	3	D.Garforth
Lock	4	M.Johnson (c)
Lock	5	B.Kay
Flanker	6	M.Corry
Flanker	7	N.Back
No.8	8	W.Johnson

Replacements: A.Balding, G.Chuter, G.Gelderbloom, F.Tournaire, J.Kronfeld, H.Ellis, S.Vesty

Leicester Tigers crashed out of the Heineken Cup after losing to Munster.

Welford Road came alive as passionate supporters from both sides flooded into the ground. The extended seating in the Clubhouse Stand added to the atmosphere and intensity of the game with nearly 1,000 extra seats added to Tigers' 16,845 capacity.

> "As far as we were concerned, the heart and soul was there, but we made some unforced errors and wrong decisions in key areas." – **Dean Richards**

Defence was solid in the first half with the only points coming from the boot of Munster fly half Ronan O'Gara, who scored one penalty from two. Tigers were unable to benefit from their majority possession and failed to capitalise on three attempts at goal.

However, they did well to keep an eager Munster side from crossing their line in the first 40 minutes

20   Munster

Tries: O'Gara, Stringer   **Cons:** O'Gara (2)
                      Pens: O'Gara (2)

after the Irishmen tested Tigers with a concentrated series of scrums, lineouts and rolling mauls in their 22. Defence from both sides held up to leave the half-time score at 3-0 to Munster.

The home side looked to make an impression early in the second half and in the first 20 minutes they penetrated the Munster line and converted to put seven points on the board. The pack rallied down the left side of the pitch before passing wide to Geordan Murphy on the right, setting up a two on one for Steve Booth who sold the dummy to the Munster wing and took the inside shoulder to dive over the line. Tim Stimpson converted to take Tigers into a 7-6 lead.

O'Gara added to a further penalty with a converted try after nearly 30 minutes. Scrum half Peter Stringer added a late try, converted by O'Gara, to leave the final score at 20-7 to Munster.

Position	No.	Player
Full Back	15	J.Staunton
Right Wing	14	J.Kelly
Centre	13	M.Mullins
Centre	12	R.Henderson
Left Wing	11	A.Horgan
Fly Half	10	R.O'Gara
Scrum Half	9	P.Stringer
Prop	1	J.Hayes
Hooker	2	F.Sheahan
Prop	3	M.Horan
Lock	4	D.O'Callaghan
Lock	5	P.O'Connell
Flanker	6	J.Williams (c)
Flanker	7	A.Quinlan
No.8	8	A.Foley

Replacements: J.Blaney, J.Holland, S.Kerr, D.Leamy, D.Malone, M.O'Driscoll, D.Crotty

Did you know?

Prior to this match Munster have played Tigers just twice before - in April 2000 when they lost 17-25 at Welford Road, and in the previous year's Heineken Cup final when Leicester won 15-9.

Match Stats	LEICESTER TIGERS	Munster Rugby
Tackles	45	114
Missed Tackles	6	23
Ball Carries	92	39
Metres	352	195
Defenders Beaten	14	9
Passes	142	63
Clean Breaks	6	3
Pens / Free Kicks	12	13
Turnovers	24	9
Breakdowns Won	82	35
% Line-Outs Won	65	83
% Scrums Won	100	83

NEC Harlequins 17

Tries: Gollings
Pens: Burke [3] **DGs:** Burke

Position	No.	Player
Full Back	15	N.Williams
Right Wing	14	D.Luger
Centre	13	W.Greenwood
Centre	12	M.Deane
Left Wing	11	B.Gollings
Fly Half	10	P.Burke
Scrum Half	9	B.Fulton
Prop	1	C.Jones
Hooker	2	T.Fuga
Prop	3	J.Leonard
Lock	4	B.Davison
Lock	5	S.Miall
Flanker	6	A.Tiatia
Flanker	7	A.Vos (c)
No.8	8	T.Diprose

Replacements: S.Bemand, J.Dawson, R.Jewell, K.Rudzki, L.Sherriff, R.Winters, V.Satala

Leicester Tigers went down 17-9 to Harlequins at The Stoop – the visitors' first league loss at the Twickenham ground for 11 years.

After a disappointing display the previous week against Munster, Tim Stimpson was back on form and brought in nine points for Tigers in the first half, after they had taken a 6-0 lead in the first twenty minutes.

Harlequins picked up the only try of the game after winning a scrum in the Leicester half. A poorly judged pass by centre Will Greenwood was picked up by team mate Ben Gollings who chipped the ball past Geordan Murphy and outpaced Stimpson to take the score.

> "You can't always be successful...at some stage you are going to have a hiccup."
> **– Dean Richards**

Tigers struggled to threaten the Quins line and the home team looked dangerous towards the end of the half. Tigers No.10 Sam Vesty stopped them from scoring when he touched down in his own try area, just keeping Greenwood off the score, to leave Tigers going into the break 9-5 up.

Leicester were unable to turn pressure into points in the second half and did not captalise on an Ace Tiatia sin bin in the last quarter.

As Harlequins sought to clear themselves from the relegation zone they had more to play for and scored all the points after the break.

Did you know?
The Quins gained just 30 points in the league at home in the 2002/03 season placing them ninth in the 'home' league table.

9 Leicester Tigers

Pens: Stimpson (3)

Paul Burke added three penalties in the second forty and a last-minute drop goal to keep Tigers from even gaining a bonus point for losing by less than seven points.

Match Stats	NEC HARLEQUINS	LEICESTER TIGERS
Tackles	142	65
Missed Tackles	21	12
Ball Carries	64	105
Metres	299	552
Defenders Beaten	12	14
Passes	105	155
Clean Breaks	3	4
Pens / Free Kicks	10	12
Turnovers	12	17
Breakdowns Won	54	93
% Line-Outs Won	72	94
% Scrums Won	100	100

Position	No.	Player
Full Back	15	T.Stimpson
Right Wing	14	G.Murphy
Centre	13	L.Lloyd
Centre	12	R.Kafer
Left Wing	11	F.Tuilagi
Fly Half	10	S.Vesty
Scrum Half	9	H.Ellis
Prop	1	P.Cook
Hooker	2	D.West
Prop	3	D.Garforth
Lock	4	M.Johnson (c)
Lock	5	B.Kay
Flanker	6	M.Corry
Flanker	7	J.Kronfeld
No.8	8	A.Balding

Replacements: S.Booth, G.Gelderbloom, G.Chuter, L.Deacon, R.Nebbett, P.Short, T.Tierney

Leicester Tigers   18

Pens: Booth (5), McMullen

Position	No.	Player
Full Back	15	G.Murphy
Right Wing	14	G.Raynor
Centre	13	L.Lloyd
Centre	12	F.Tuilagi
Left Wing	11	S.Booth
Fly Half	10	C.McMullen
Scrum Half	9	H.Ellis
Prop	1	P.Freshwater
Hooker	2	G.Chuter
Prop	3	D.Garforth
Lock	4	M.Johnson (c)
Lock	5	L.Deacon
Flanker	6	M.Corry
Flanker	7	W.Skinner
No.8	8	A.Balding

Replacements: P.Cook, G.Gelderbloom, J.Hamilton, R.Kafer, B.Kay, R.Nebbett, L.Abraham

Leicester Tigers moved closer to securing a place in next year's Heineken Cup with a nail-biting win over Leeds Tykes at a sell-out Welford Road.

There was everything to play for with both teams fighting for the number four spot and the possibility of a place in the top three.

> "It was an important win when you consider the amount of players we had out – about 11 or 12. We still had confidence in the players we fielded but injuries cause disruptions in training."
> **– Dean Richards**

An injury-plagued Tigers squad was diminished even further in the week prior to the game with Dorian West unavailable for selection after injuring his calf in training, meaning that Will Skinner became the seventh Tigers academy player this year to make his first team debut. The 19-year-old started at number seven and was praised by Dean Richards after the match.

In a match decided by penalties, the only try came courtesy of Tykes winger George Harder who crossed the line 25 minutes into the first half.

Tigers' makeshift place kicker, Steve Booth, got an almost clean sheet, kicking five from six penalties before being stretchered off just before the break after falling awkwardly into a tackle.

The home side's defence held up despite some serious threats from the Tykes in the second half with Harder nearly crossing the line, but for a try-saving tackle by scrum half Harry Ellis.

Tigers set up some excellent attack play throughout the game and full back Geordan Murphy's well-aimed kicks earned Tigers territory, but poor handling let the

17   Leeds Tykes

Tries: Harder
Pens: Van Straaten (4)

side down at the crunch point with knock-ons losing them possession.

Freddie Tuilagi was awarded the Bollinger Champagne Tackle of the Match for his great defensive work in the centre and Gareth Raynor looked dangerous with ball in hand on the wing.

Ellis was back on form at scrum half and his dynamic play almost paid off after he chipped through a ball into Tykes' 22 and nearly outran the defender.

Fly half Craig McMullen took over the kicking duties in the second half to add Tigers' only three points of the 40 minutes and leave the final score at 18-17 to the home side.

Did you know?
This was Leicester Tigers' 100th win in the Premiership since the competition began in 1997/1998, making them the first team to clock up the century. The Tykes' two previous visits to Welford Road were for the Tetley's Bitter Cup 5th round in January 1999 (lost 0-49) and in the Premiership last April (lost 10-31).

Position	No.	Player
Full Back	15	D.Albanese
Right Wing	14	G.Harder
Centre	13	T.Davies
Centre	12	B.Van Straaten
Left Wing	11	W.Stanley
Fly Half	10	G.Ross
Scrum Half	9	D.Hegarty
Prop	1	J.Wring
Hooker	2	M.Regan (c)
Prop	3	M.Holt
Lock	4	C.Murphy
Lock	5	T.Palmer
Flanker	6	C.Mather
Flanker	7	D.Hyde
No.8	8	A.Popham

Replacements: A.Dickens, C.Emmerson, I.Feau'nati, C.Hall, G.Kerr, P.Murphy, R.Rawlinson

Match Stats	LEICESTER TIGERS	LEEDS TYKES
Tackles	63	64
Missed Tackles	12	10
Ball Carries	57	47
Metres	257	177
Defenders Beaten	18	14
Passes	78	58
Clean Breaks	0	5
Pens / Free Kicks	7	14
Turnovers	11	10
Breakdowns Won	57	45
% Line-Outs Won	88	92
% Scrums Won	94	100

April Review

Tigers started the month with a promising 33-20 victory over Sale Sharks at Welford Road, putting the team in with a chance of reaching the top three, and building up hopes for the following week's fixture against Munster in the Heineken Cup quarter-finals.

The Munster match was probably Tigers' most hyped game of the season with ticket allocation arguments between the club, ERC and Munster intensifying this repeat of the previous year's final.

Welford Road's capacity increased to 17,600 to accommodate as many supporters as possible but an almost gridlocked game meant that Tigers were only able to put one try past the visitors and Munster won the match 20-7.

Snippets

Former Tigers star Matt Poole completed the London Marathon in 4 hours and 24 minutes, raising over £7,000 for the Wooden Spoon Society.

Flo Gas team up with Tigers as rugby course sponsors for 2003 and Academy Vice Presidents.

Welford Road hosts its largest crowd in the professional era, welcoming 17,600 supporters for the Heineken Cup quarter-final against Munster.

Results (Leicester Tigers' score first)

Apr 4	ZP	Sharks	H	33-20
Apr 13	HC	Munster	H	7-20
Apr 19	ZP	NEC Harlequins	A	9-17
Apr 26	ZP	Leeds Tykes	H	18-17

Key

ZP	Zurich Premiership
ZW	Zurich Wildcard
HC	Heineken Cup
PGC	Powergen Cup

ZURICH PREMIERSHIP

Team	P	W	D	L	F	A	PD	BP	Pts
Gloucester	20	16	2	2	563	353	+210	8	76
London Wasps	20	12	2	6	516	426	+90	10	62
Sharks	20	12	2	6	528	420	+108	9	61
Leicester Tigers	20	12	0	8	416	345	+71	6	54
Northampton Saints	20	11	0	9	453	351	+102	9	53
Leeds Tykes	20	11	2	7	442	384	+58	5	53
NEC Harlequins	20	8	0	12	417	508	-91	8	40
Newcastle Falcons	20	7	0	13	350	499	-149	7	35
Saracens	19	6	0	13	426	526	-100	8	32
Bath Rugby	20	6	2	12	341	448	-107	4	32
London Irish	20	6	1	13	371	445	-74	5	31
Bristol Shoguns	19	6	1	12	437	555	-118	5	31

April Review

Top Points Scorers

Name	Total
T.Stimpson	150
G.Murphy	53
S.Booth	42
J.Kronfeld	25
O.Smith	20
L.Lloyd	15

Top Try Scorers

Name	Total
G.Murphy	5
J.Kronfeld	5
S.Booth	4
O.Smith	4
L.Lloyd	3
D.West	3

Top Penalty Scorers

Name	Total
T.Stimpson	34
S.Booth	6
G.Murphy	5
S.Vesty	2
C.McMullen	1

Top Drop Goal Scorers

Name	Tries
G.Murphy	1
T.Stimpson	1
A.Healey	1

Regular season matches only

Player Of The Month

Geordan Murphy

Following hot in Josh's footsteps, Geordan became the second player to get the award twice in the same season. Dynamic performances for both his club and country secured Geordan the vote this month.

In April, Geordan was shocked to also be named Player of the Season by Tigers members at the annual awards dinner.

Matches	3
Ball Carries	20
Metres	121
Defenders Beaten	8
Clean Breaks	3
Tackles	2
Missed Tackles	0
Try Passes	3
Tries Scored	1

Leicester Tigers   19

Tries: Holtby, Stimpson
Pens: Stimpson (2) **DGs:** Murphy

Position	No.	Player
Full Back	15	T.Stimpson
Right Wing	14	J.Holtby
Centre	13	L.Lloyd
Centre	12	F.Tuilagi
Left Wing	11	G.Murphy
Fly Half	10	C.McMullen
Scrum Half	9	H.Ellis
Prop	1	P.Freshwater
Hooker	2	G.Chuter
Prop	3	D.Garforth
Lock	4	M.Johnson (c)
Lock	5	L.Deacon
Flanker	6	M.Corry
Flanker	7	W.Skinner
No.8	8	A.Balding

Replacements: L.Abraham, J.Hamilton, G.Gelderbloom, R.Kafer, R.Nebbett, G.Rowntree, B.Kay

For the second match in a row, a Leicester Tigers match was decided by a single point, only this time it was not in their favour in an infuriating match at Welford Road.

The first half looked promising with a Tim Stimpson try after just four minutes. The pacey full back joined the line to take a miss pass from fly half Craig McMullen and slice through the Irish defence to score left of the posts.

> "In the first half we looked promising, while in the second half we never turned up." – **Dean Richards**

The half continued with little inspiration from Tigers, with the team choosing to run with ball rather than kick for territory.

London Irish were no better but benefitted from ill discipline from Tigers, who gave away four easy penalties for ace boot Mark Mapletoft to convert.

On the half-hour mark, Tigers upped the pace and in a flash of brilliance winger John Holtby scored in

20 London Irish

Tries: Worsley
Pens: Mapletoft (5)

the corner. McMullen set up the score and quick hands through Freddie Tuilagi and Leon Lloyd fed the ball to the youngster who touched down over the line.

In injury time, London Irish fought back to extend their lead with a try courtesy of Mike Worsley. Tigers answered back with a Geordan Murphy drop goal, leaving the half-time score at 17-13 to Irish.

The second half didn't live up to expectations and neither team could breach the opposition defence. Tigers took the lead in the last quarter after Stimpson cleared two penalties, but the home side gave away a penalty in front of the posts for Mapletoft to fire Irish into the lead with just ten minutes to go.

Tigers made a last ditch attempt to take the lead, but despite some strong runs by Adam Balding and replacement flanker Luke Abraham, the side's efforts went unrewarded and the final score stayed at 20-19 to London Irish.

Position	No.	Player
Full Back	15	M.Horak
Right Wing	14	P.Sackey
Centre	13	G.Appleford
Centre	12	R.Hoadley
Left Wing	11	K.Barrett
Fly Half	10	M.Mapletoft
Scrum Half	9	H.Martens
Prop	1	M.Worsley
Hooker	2	A.Flavin
Prop	3	R.Hardwick
Lock	4	R.Strudwick (c)
Lock	5	R.Casey
Flanker	6	D.Danagher
Flanker	7	K.Dawson
No.8	8	C.Sheasby

Replacements: K.Brennan, B.Everitt, S.Halford, N.Hatley, N.Kennedy, K.Roche, E.Thrower

Did you know?

On this day Mark Mapletoft took his career points tally against Leicester to 148. Only Rob Andrew (186) and Paul Grayson (169) have scored more.

Match Stats	TIGERS	
Tackles	64	137
Missed Tackles	13	17
Ball Carries	108	64
Metres	470	412
Defenders Beaten	9	15
Passes	143	102
Clean Breaks	7	0
Pens / Free Kicks	7	15
Turnovers	10	9
Breakdowns Won	88	59
% Line-Outs Won	86	78
% Scrums Won	100	92

Date: Saturday 10th May 2003

Gloucester 31

Tries: Delport, Beim, Gomersall, Fanolua
Cons: Mercier (4) **Pens:** Mercier

Position	No.	Player
Full Back	15	T.Delport
Right Wing	14	M.Garvey
Centre	13	T.Fanolua
Centre	12	H.Paul
Left Wing	11	T.Beim
Fly Half	10	L.Mercier
Scrum Half	9	A.Gomersall
Prop	1	T.Woodman
Hooker	2	O.Azam
Prop	3	A.Deacon
Lock	4	A.Eustace
Lock	5	M.Cornwell
Flanker	6	J.Boer (c)
Flanker	7	A.Hazell
No.8	8	J.Paramore

Replacements: S.Amor, P.Buxton, C.Collins, R.Fidler, C.Stuart-Smith, R.Todd, P.Vickery

Leicester Tigers rounded off the regular season with a defeat at top of the table Gloucester.

Tigers started brightly with a series of impressive forward surges as their pack showed the form that had been missing in recent weeks.

Recalled flanker Peter Short, prop Graham Rowntree, skipper Martin Johnson and number eight Adam Balding drove into the Gloucester defence on numerous occasions, but the visitors' back division failed to capitalise.

"It was an enthralling contest - except the last try. Though I was not happy with the result." – **Dean Richards**

Gloucester took a 10-0 lead courtesy of a counter-attacking try from South African full back Thinus Delport, converted by fly half Ludovic Mercier who also added a penalty.

Tigers then rallied to draw level as full back Geordan Murphy kicked a good penalty and centre Freddie Tuilagi accepted the gift of a pass from the

13 Leicester Tigers

Tries: Tuilagi **Cons:** Murphy
Pens: Murphy (2)

opposition to sprint under the posts from 30 metres.

Murphy added the extras and just as it seemed it would be all-square at the break, the visitors lost the ball in Gloucester's 22 and another excellent counter-attack resulted in a try in the left hand corner by former England winger Tom Beim. Mercier, playing his last match in front of the Kingsholm faithful, converted effortlessly from the touchline to give his side a 17-10 half-time lead.

Tigers started the second half in the same manner as they had the first, and forward dominance gave Murphy an easy penalty chance to draw back to 17-13. Sadly, that was the end of their scoring opportunities as the home side remained solid in defence. Gloucester scored two tries in the final quarter from centre Terry Fanolua and scrum half Andy Gomersall, with Mercier converting both.

The result meant that Tigers would have to beat Harlequins in a two-legged Zurich Wildcard semi-final to qualify for next season's Heineken Cup.

Did you know?
Gloucester's solitary win against Leicester in the last six premiership meetings was 22-13 at Kingshom on March 31 2001.

Position	No.	Player
Full Back	15	G.Murphy
Right Wing	14	J.Holtby
Centre	13	L.Lloyd
Centre	12	F.Tuilagi
Left Wing	11	H.Ellis
Fly Half	10	C.McMullen
Scrum Half	9	J.Hamilton
Prop	1	G.Rowntree
Hooker	2	G.Chuter
Prop	3	D.Garforth
Lock	4	M.Johnson (c)
Lock	5	B.Kay
Flanker	6	P.Short
Flanker	7	J.Kronfeld
No.8	8	A.Balding

Replacements: L.Deacon, P.Freshwater, G.Gelderbloom, R.Nebbett, W.Skinner, T.Tierney, R.Kafer

Match Stats	GLOUCESTER RFC	LEICESTER TIGERS
Tackles	125	30
Missed Tackles	18	16
Ball Carries	40	101
Metres	413	404
Defenders Beaten	20	16
Passes	87	128
Clean Breaks	8	7
Pens / Free Kicks	18	8
Turnovers	14	20
Breakdowns Won	18	90
% Line-Outs Won	77	95
% Scrums Won	10	82

NEC Harlequins   26

Tries: Fuga, Deane **Cons:** Burke (2)
Pens: Burke (3) **DGs:** Burke

Position	No.	Player
Full Back	15	N.Williams
Right Wing	14	U.Monye
Centre	13	W.Greenwood
Centre	12	M.Deane
Left Wing	11	D.Luger
Fly Half	10	P.Burke
Scrum Half	9	M.Powell
Prop	1	J.Leonard
Hooker	2	T.Fuga
Prop	3	L.Gomez
Lock	4	B.Davison
Lock	5	S.Miall
Flanker	6	R.Winters
Flanker	7	A.Vos (c)
No.8	8	T.Diprose

Replacements: S.Bemand, J.Evans, B.Gollings, J.Hayter, C.Jones, K.Rudzki, P.Sanderson

Despite staging a remarkable final quarter comeback at the Stoop, Leicester Tigers just failed to gain an advantage for the second leg of the Zurich Wildcard semi-final.

Tigers had started strongly in a tight opening 20 minutes, taking the lead when full back Tim Stimpson celebrated his recovery form injury with a penalty, after Mel Deane had chopped down Glenn Gelderbloom with a high tackle.

Quins hit straight back however, and hooker Tani Fuga went over in the left hand corner after a break by former Tigers centre Will Greenwood. Fly half Paul Burke added the extras to take his side into a 7-3 lead.

"I was disappointed with the fact that we gave two soft tries away and conceded three stupid penalties but was pleased with the fact that we came back from a 17-point deficit to almost snatch victory. I don't know if it's advantage Leicester or not." – **Dean Richards**

23   Leicester Tigers

Tries: Corry, Murphy **Cons:** Stimpson (2)
Pens: Stimpson (3)

The home side's second try came from a fine chip ahead from Matt Powell which Deane was first to touch down.

Burke again converted from wide out before adding a penalty to take his side into half-time with a 17-3 lead.

Stimpson and Burke exchanged penalties at the start of the second period and a drop goal from the Irish outside half took his side into a commanding 17-point lead at 23-6.

Tigers brought on Martin Johnson, Graham Rowntree, Darren Garforth, Dorian West and Will Skinner and they provided the platform for a stirring comeback.

Tigers full back Geordan Murphy had looked dangerous with the ball in hand all evening and he finally got on the score sheet with a fine break past three Quins defenders.

Burke kicked another penalty but Tigers weren't finished and Martin Corry barged over the line from close range with five minutes left on the clock.

Stimpson converted and added an injury time penalty to reduce the arrears to just three points.

Position	No.	Player
Full Back	15	T.Stimpson
Right Wing	14	G.Murphy
Centre	13	G.Gelderbloom
Centre	12	F.Tuilagi
Left Wing	11	L.Lloyd
Fly Half	10	C.McMullen
Scrum Half	9	H.Ellis
Prop	1	P.Freshwater
Hooker	2	G.Chuter
Prop	3	R.Nebbett
Lock	4	L.Deacon
Lock	5	M.Corry
Flanker	6	P.Short
Flanker	7	J.Kronfeld
No.8	8	A.Balding

Replacements: D.Garforth, J.Hamilton, M.Johnson, G.Rowntree, W.Skinner, S.Vesty, D.West

Match Stats	NEC HARLEQUINS	LEICESTER TIGERS
Tackles	92	63
Missed Tackles	15	12
Ball Carries	44	81
Metres	290	394
Defenders Beaten	15	17
Passes	3	4
Clean Breaks	2	2
Pens / Free Kicks	10	12
Turnovers	11	16
Breakdowns Won	35	59
% Line-Outs Won	75	75
% Scrums Won	100	100

Leicester Tigers　　　28

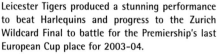

Tries: Back, Gelderbloom, Skinner **Cons:** Stimpson (2)
Pens: Stimpson (3) - (Leicester Tigers win 51-39 on aggregate)

Position	No.	Player
Full Back	15	T.Stimpson
Right Wing	14	G.Murphy
Centre	13	G.Gelderbloom
Centre	12	F.Tuilagi
Left Wing	11	L.Lloyd
Fly Half	10	C.McMullen
Scrum Half	9	H.Ellis
Prop	1	G.Rowntree
Hooker	2	D.West
Prop	3	R.Nebbett
Lock	4	M.Johnson (c)
Lock	5	L.Deacon
Flanker	6	P.Short
Flanker	7	N.Back
No.8	8	M.Corry

Replacements: A.Balding, P.Freshwater, D.Garforth, J.Hamilton, S.Vesty, B.Kay, W.Skinner

Leicester Tigers produced a stunning performance to beat Harlequins and progress to the Zurich Wildcard Final to battle for the Premiership's last European Cup place for 2003-04.

Tigers started promisingly with an energetic five minutes but the side's hard work failed to pay off and Harlequins picked up three points on their only foray into the Tigers half.

> "I was more than happy when Back came off to put Will Skinner on. He has acquitted himself well over the last few weeks. I thought his score was critical. Freddie Tuilagi has played outstandingly well and made the half-break and for Will to finish off was probably fitting."
> **– Dean Richards**

Two missed Stimpson penalties meant that Tigers were unable to capitalise on their majority possession and it wasn't until the end of the first quarter that the full back atoned for his earlier mistakes and put some points on the board, levelling the scores.

Tigers continued to dominate the match but a lapse in concentration allowed Harlequins' speedy winger Ugo Monye to carve through the Tigers defence and gallop over the line unopposed. Paul Burke converted.

Tigers were soon back in the Harlequins half and threatening their line with some strong forward play, but the defence wouldn't give and it was an error by the visitors that eventually gave Tigers their chance.

A poor line-out fell into the hands of Graham Rowntree and the ball found its way to Glenn Gelderbloom, who slipped through a gap in the defence to run in Tigers' first try of the

13   **NEC Harlequins**

Tries: Monye **Cons:** Burke
Pens: Burke (2)

match. Stimpson converted to increase the home side's narrow lead and take the half-time score to 13-10 to Tigers.

Tigers started the second half well and Stimpson picked up an easy three points in the first five minutes.

Just under 20 minutes into the half, Tigers' controlled attack earned the team a second try. Freddie Tuilagi set the move up with help from Darren Garforth who saw the ball into the Harlequins 22. Leon Lloyd took over the charge before pivoting the ball back down the line and into the hands of Neil Back, who stepped back inside and wriggled over the line for a score.

Ten minutes later Tuilagi set up another charge into the Harlequins 22 but was tackled short of the line. Replacement flanker Will Skinner was in close support and took the ball from Tuilagi to run in his debut first team try.

Stimpson had an easy conversion to secure Tigers' Wildcard Final spot with a final score of 28-13 in their favour.

Position	No.	Player
Full Back	15	N.Williams
Right Wing	14	U.Monye
Centre	13	W.Greenwood
Centre	12	M.Deane
Left Wing	11	D.Luger
Fly Half	10	P.Burke
Scrum Half	9	M.Powell
Prop	1	J.Leonard
Hooker	2	T.Fuga
Prop	3	J.Dawson
Lock	4	B.Davison
Lock	5	S.Miall
Flanker	6	R.Winters
Flanker	7	A.Vos (c)
No.8	8	T.Diprose

Replacements: S.Bemand, J.Evans, B.Gollings, L.Gomez, J.Hayter, K.Rudzki, P.Sanderson

Match Stats	LEICESTER TIGERS	NEC HARLEQUINS
Tackles	49	108
Missed Tackles	14	23
Ball Carries	87	36
Metres	370	212
Defenders Beaten	20	13
Passes	122	74
Clean Breaks	6	4
Pens / Free Kicks	6	10
Turnovers	15	13
Breakdowns Won	79	33
% Line-Outs Won	85	78
% Scrums Won	100	92

Leicester Tigers 27

Tries: West, Back **Cons:** Stimpson
Pens: Stimpson (4) **DGs:** McMullen - (Leicester Tigers win after extra time)

Position	No.	Player
Full Back	15	T.Stimpson
Right Wing	14	J.Holtby
Centre	13	G.Gelderbloom
Centre	12	F.Tuilagi
Left Wing	11	L.Lloyd
Fly Half	10	C.McMullen
Scrum Half	9	H.Ellis
Prop	1	G.Rowntree
Hooker	2	D.West
Prop	3	D.Garforth
Lock	4	M.Johnson (c)
Lock	5	B.Kay
Flanker	6	P.Short
Flanker	7	N.Back
No.8	8	M.Corry

Replacements: G.Chuter, P.Freshwater, W.Skinner, S.Vesty, R.Nebbett, A.Balding, J.Hamilton

Leicester Tigers clinched the final Heineken Cup spot for next season in a nail-biting Zurich Wildcard Final at Franklin's Gardens.

With temperatures touching 80 degrees the two sides found themselves locked at 20-20 after normal time and were forced to play 20 minutes of energy-sapping extra time. Veteran flanker Neil Back was the hero as he crashed over from a maul deep in Saracens' 22 five minutes from the end, saving the players and 8,000 supporters from the prospect of a penalty shoot-out.

Saracens had taken an early lead, nearly two hours earlier, courtesy of a try from Richard Hill who seized on a Ben Kay tap-down from a line-out.

Former Tiger Andy Goode converted in reply to a solitary Tim Stimpson penalty for a 7-3 lead.

Stimpson missed two further shots at goal but then regained the initiative with two successful strikes for a 9-7 advantage. Goode had the final word in the half however, with his first penalty for a 10-9 interval lead.

> "We made a lot of errors – many of which were heat induced and the pressure of the day – but the fact they came through showed the character of the side." – **Dean Richards**

The Tigers' pack took a stranglehold in the second period and an offside decision against two Saracens defenders earned them a penalty in a dangerous position. Skipper Martin Johnson showed great nerve to turn down the three points on offer and go for the try. Stimpson kicked to touch and Johnson himself claimed the resulting line-out before his forwards mustered a massive drive for the line.

The maul moved left and right but always forwards and when it collapsed over the line, hooker Dorian West emerged from under the pile of bodies with the ball. The 35-year-old threw the ball into the crowd in delight and deservedly so after an all-action performance in the searing heat.

Stimpson failed with the conversion attempt but more forward pressure and a series of powerful drives

20

Saracens

Tries: Hill, Haughten **Cons:** Goode (2)
Pens: Goode (2)

by centre Freddie Tuilagi set up another promising field position in front of the Saracens posts.

This time fly half Craig McMullen moved back deep into the pocket and opted for the drop goal which gave Tigers a commanding 17-10 lead.

Saracens weren't finished however, and a missed touch kick from Stimpson gave winger Darragh O'Mahony the chance to launch a counter-attack. He fed replacement full back Thomas Castaignede and the Frenchman committed two defenders before giving flyer Richard Haughton the chance to outstrip the Leicester defence.

Goode's conversion levelled the scores at 17-17 but Tigers came roaring back when another barnstorming run from Tuilagi resulted in a penalty right in front of the Saracens posts. Stimpson stroked it over, but the drama was not over as Ben Kay was penalised for obstruction at the restart, giving Goode the chance to level from 45 metres.

Referee Roy Maybank kept the tension going with nine minutes of injury time before eventually signalling for extra time. The first period was scoreless but then came Back's clincher and a place in Europe's premier club competition.

Position	No.	Player
Full Back	15	T.Horan
Right Wing	14	R.Haughton
Centre	13	B.Johnston
Centre	12	K.Sorrell
Left Wing	11	D.O'Mahony
Fly Half	10	A.Goode
Scrum Half	9	K.Bracken
Prop	1	D.Flatman
Hooker	2	M.Cairns
Prop	3	C.Califano
Lock	4	A.Benazzi
Lock	5	C.Yandell (c)
Flanker	6	K.Chesney
Flanker	7	R.Hill
No.8	8	B.Skirving

Replacements: T.Castaignede, D.Kirton, N.Little, A.Roques, R.Russell, B.Russell, M.Storey

Match Stats	TIGERS	SARACENS
Tackles	72	129
Missed Tackles	15	19
Ball Carries	98	63
Metres	454	289
Defenders Beaten	14	15
Passes	115	104
Clean Breaks	8	5
Pens / Free Kicks	11	11
Turnovers	18	19
Breakdowns Won	93	58
% Line-Outs Won	89	64
% Scrums Won	100	91

May Review

The last month of the season was Tigers' busiest with five matches, including two in one week against Harlequins in the Zurich Wildcard Playoffs.

Tigers performed poorly at the start of the month, losing to London Irish at home and then to Gloucester and Harlequins away. But the team pulled it out where it counted and beat Harlequins convincingly in the return leg of the Wildcard Playoffs, going on to beat Saracens in extra time of the Zurich Wildcard Final and qualifying for a place in the Heineken Cup 2003/04.

May was also a busy month for player recruitment as Dean Richards announced four international signings in the form of Ramiro Pez, Darren Morris, Daryl Gibson and Julian White.

Tigers U21s were the stars of the month, and were crowned Zurich U21s champions after a thrilling match at Welford Road where they thrashed Gloucester by seven tries to one.

Off the pitch, Tigers welcomed the millionth Premiership fan to Welford Road at the London Irish game and celebrated their eleventh sell-out of the season.

Snippets

Tigers' new home shirt is more successful than ever as it crashes through the 1,000 sales barrier just 10 days after its release.

Peter Wheeler is honoured at the Professional Rugby Players Association Awards when he is inducted into the PRA Gerrard Hall of Fame.

Welford Road welcomes over 4,000 Leicester students for the annual Varsity match, won 30-25 by De Montfort University.

Results (Leicester Tigers' score first)						Key	
May 3	ZP	London Irish	H	19-20		ZP	Zurich Premiership
May 10	ZP	Gloucester	A	13-31		ZW	Zurich Wildcard
May 14	ZW	NEC Harlequins	A	23-26		HC	Heineken Cup
May 18	ZW	NEC Harlequins	H	28-13		PGC	Powergen Cup
May 31	ZW	Saracens	N	27-20			

Team	P	W	D	L	F	A	PD	BP	Pts
Gloucester	22	17	2	3	617	396	+221	10	82
London Wasps	22	13	2	7	553	460	+93	11	67
Northampton Saints	22	13	0	9	512	376	+136	10	62
Sharks	22	12	2	8	556	470	+86	10	62
Leeds Tykes	22	12	2	8	478	435	+43	6	58
Leicester Tigers	22	12	0	10	448	396	+52	7	55
NEC Harlequins	22	9	0	13	461	560	-99	8	44
Saracens	22	8	0	14	499	587	-88	10	42
London Irish	22	8	1	13	432	485	-53	6	40
Newcastle Falcons	22	8	0	14	388	545	-157	8	40
Bath Rugby	22	7	2	13	385	490	-105	4	36
Bristol Shoguns	22	7	1	14	504	633	-129	6	36

May Review

Top Points Scorers

Name	Total
T.Stimpson	161
G.Murphy	64
S.Booth	42
J.Kronfeld	25
O.Smith	20
L.Lloyd	15

Top Try Scorers

Name	Total
G.Murphy	5
J.Kronfeld	5
S.Booth	4
O.Smith	4
L.Lloyd	3
D.West	3

Player Of The Month

Darren Garforth

In a fitting tribute to one of Leicester Tigers' greatest servants, Darren Garforth was named player of the month for May.

Darren retired at the end of the season after 12 years service to the club. The stalwart prop made 346 appearances for Tigers since making his debut against the Northern Division in September 1991 and was the first player in the country to clock up 200 appearances in the English Premiership.

Appearances	2
Tackles	6
Missed Tackles	1
Ball Carries	10
Metres	20
Defenders Beaten	0
Clean Breaks	0
Tries Scored	0

Top Penalty Scorers

Name	Total
T.Stimpson	36
G.Murphy	7
S.Booth	6
S.Vesty	2
C.McMullen	1

Top Drop Goal Scorers

Name	Total
G.Murphy	2
T.Stimpson	1
A.Healey	1

Regular season matches only

2002-03 Season Stats

Key: **App** - Appearances **T** - Tries
Rep - Replacements **SLT** - Since Last Try

Squad	2002-03 Season								Leicester First XV Career								
	All Games				Zurich Prem				All Games				League Games				
	App	Rep	T	Pts	App	Rep	T	Pts	App	Rep	T	Pts	App	Rep	T	Pts	SLT
L.Abraham	0	2	-	-	0	1	-	-	0	2	-	-	0	1	-	-	-
N.Back	16	6	7	35	8	5	3	15	274	16	108	530	165	12	64	319	1
A.Balding	15	9	1	5	10	3	-	-	39	54	4	20	25	30	2	10	17
S.Booth	17	12	10	72	12	7	4	42	45	18	26	173	31	12	16	123	3
G.Chuter	11	13	2	10	7	8	-	-	15	24	2	10	9	15	-	-	8
P.Cook	1	-	-	-	1	-	-	-	1	-	-	-	1	-	-	-	-
M.Corry	33	-	3	15	20	-	1	5	156	9	16	80	98	7	9	45	3
L.Deacon	17	2	1	5	10	1	-	-	49	8	2	10	30	6	1	5	12
H.Ellis	19	4	5	25	13	1	3	15	31	19	7	35	21	11	3	15	10
P.Freshwater	14	9	1	5	9	5	-	-	64	73	8	40	25	49	1	5	18
D.Garforth	19	10	-	-	13	5	-	-	325	21	19	90	196	10	7	34	43
G.Gelderbloom	8	10	1	5	2	8	-	-	30	33	3	15	17	20	2	10	2
B.Gerry	0	1	-	-	0	1	-	-	0	1	-	-	0	1	-	-	-
J.Hamilton	10	12	2	10	6	6	1	5	127	57	24	118	63	32	7	35	10
A.Healey	12	-	3	23	6	-	2	13	154	14	45	246	101	11	27	145	2
D.Hipkiss	2	1	1	5	1	-	-	-	2	1	1	5	1	1	-	-	3
J.Holtby	6	1	1	5	4	-	1	5	6	2	1	5	4	1	1	5	3
D.Jelley	4	-	-	-	2	-	-	-	100	45	21	105	41	27	2	10	11
M.Johnson	29	3	-	-	19	-	-	-	301	10	15	75	187	4	8	40	45
W.Johnson	13	2	-	-	7	1	-	-	106	32	7	35	58	18	1	5	59
R.Kafer	22	-	4	23	14	-	3	15	53	1	8	43	33	-	6	30	4
B.Kay	19	8	2	10	11	6	1	5	98	18	7	35	58	12	5	25	10
J.Kronfeld	21	6	7	35	14	4	5	25	36	10	9	45	24	6	7	35	8

Squad	2002-03 Season – All Games				2002-03 Season – Zurich Prem				Leicester First XV Career – All Games				Leicester First XV Career – League Games				
	App	Rep	T	Pts	App	Rep	T	Pts	App	Rep	T	Pts	App	Rep	T	Pts	SLT
L.Lloyd	27	1	5	25	15	1	3	15	160	15	59	295	99	8	26	130	9
C.McMullen	8	1	-	8	5	1	-	5	8	1	-	8	5	1	-	5	-
L.Moody	8	1	1	5	6	-	-	-	94	37	18	90	63	22	9	45	3
G.Murphy	22	-	9	110	12	-	5	64	117	13	55	468	68	8	36	290	2
J.Naufahu	2	3	-	-	2	3	-	-	2	3	-	-	2	3	-	-	-
R.Nebbett	3	3	-	-	0	1	-	-	25	30	-	-	16	16	-	-	-
G.Raynor	1	3	-	-	1	2	-	-	1	3	-	-	1	2	-	-	-
G.Rowntree	16	5	1	5	10	3	1	5	299	31	17	82	169	20	4	20	18
P.Short	7	5	1	5	3	3	-	-	26	23	2	10	17	13	-	-	6
W.Skinner	2	4	1	5	2	1	-	-	2	4	1	5	2	1	-	-	2
O.Smith	19	-	6	30	13	-	4	20	52	11	17	85	33	5	8	40	3
T.Stimpson	23	2	5	278	13	1	2	161	136	9	30	1653	89	6	21	1115	4
T.Tierney	11	8	1	5	6	5	-	-	11	8	1	5	6	5	-	-	13
F.Tournaire	15	10	1	5	9	7	-	-	15	10	1	5	9	7	-	-	6
F.Tuilagi	27	-	5	25	18	2	10	61	14	-	-	70	37	3	7	35	4
S.Vesty	16	7	1	26	11	3	-	8	16	7	1	26	11	3	-	8	13
D.West	25	5	5	25	15	2	3	15	141	52	33	164	72	33	8	40	1
Total For	540	169	93	845	330	96	44	448									
Total Against			48	596			32	396									

All Games: Played 36, Won 22, Drew 1, Lost 13

League Games: Played 22, Won 12, Lost 10

2002-03 Season

Kickers	All Games					Zurich Prem		
	Miss	Succ %	Con	PG	DG	Con	P	DG
S.Booth	2	80.00	2	6	-	2	6	-
A.Healey	3	40.00	1	1	1	-	-	1
C.McMullen	1	66.67	1	1	-	1	1	-
G.Murphy	16	60.00	13	11	2	6	7	2
T.Stimpson	45	68.09	38	58	1	20	36	1
S.Vesty	8	52.94	6	3	-	1	2	-
Tigers Totals	75	65.28	61	80	5	30	52	4
Opponents	62	66.49	34	89	7	22	59	5

Leicester First XV Career

Kickers	All Games					League Games		
	Att	Succ %	Con	PG	DG	Con	PG	DG
S.Booth	19	73.68	5	9	2	5	9	2
A.Healey	10	40.00	3	1	4	2	-	2
C.McMullen	3	66.67	1	1	-	2	1	-
G.Murphy	120	64.17	47	30	3	22	20	2
T.Stimpson	832	68.63	216	355	6	142	240	2
S.Vesty	17	52.94	6	3	-	3	2	-

Key: **Con** - Conversions **PG** - Penalty Goals **DG** - Drop Goals **Att** - Attempts

Tigers Extras Review

Tigers Extras have had a mixed season but they pulled out all the stops to finish the year in triumphant style, beating Newport 57-10.

Tigers Extras combines youth and experience and is a stepping stone for many of the Tigers academy players hoping to make the move to senior rugby.

The Extras play the majority of their home fixtures at Welford Road and Tigers members can watch the matches for free with up to four guests. Non-members are also welcome and the cost of the ticket can be redeemed against a senior match.

Date: Monday 23rd September 2002	
Gloucester United	24
Tigers Extras	3

Tigers fell to a experienced Gloucester side, their spirited performance failed to justice to Tigers playing potential. Tries from Daren O'Leary and Nick Southern, were matched by consistent kicking from Simon Amor. Extras despite launching wave after wave of punishing attacks on the Gloucester defence could not convert their possession into points. With the backs initiating darting moves from all over the field. Tigers only score came from Gloucester killing the ball sending their Andy Deacon to the sin bin, and the resulting penalty converted by Luke Myring.

Date: Monday 14th October 2002	
Tigers Extras	47
Cambridge University	27

Tigers forwards were dominant in this clash with the university side. Josh Kronfeld, captain for the occasion scored a typical Tigers catch and drive try from a line. Sam Vesty converting to take the score to 7-0. Further tries were scored by scrum-half Jamie Hamilton off the back of a driving maul, Jo Naufahu and Tom Coles. Craig McMullen's Tigers debut saw him convert twice, taking the dominant Tigers well out of the oppositions grasp. However, Cambridge did not give up and had the last word with a try from lock Phil Robinson.

Date: Monday 21st October 2002	
Oxford University	10
Tigers Extras	10

A young Tigers team travelled to Oxford, and came away with a rare score draw. Both teams scored a try, conversion and penalty.

Date: Monday 2nd December 2002	
Tigers Extras	25
Harlequins	15

Tigers Extras convincingly beat the Harlequins side in a game that allowed them to showcase some of their bright new talent - including league convert Gareth Raynor. Tries from Tim Taylor, James Hamilton and Luke Abraham saw Tigers take control of the game out of Quins reach.

Date: Monday 13th January 2003	
Tigers Extras	10
Northampton Wanderers	15

Tigers Extras lost their unbeaten home record in a scrappy match against their local rivals. Each side scored two tries, but Wanderers had the edge with a successful conversion and penalty scored by the All Black sevens star Bruce Reihana. Ill discipline saw academy player Ben Gerry sin-binned, leaving the score 0-15 to the visitors. However, Extras continued to apply the pressure and continued pressure allowed the Tigers to reduce the deficit by two powerful Michael Holford tries.

Date: **Monday 10th March 2003**	
Tigers Extras	20
Gloucester United	34

Gloucester's team dynamically outperformed the Extras, in a game which saw the home side out played in the first half going into the break 17-3, with an impressive 63 metre penalty scored by full-back Tim Stimpson. The second half saw the visitors score yet another try, but the Extras continued to run at the Gloucester defence. Their perseverance was rewarded with a Gareth Raynor's first ever try for the club. The hectic pace continued for the next 10 minutes resulting in a try from Will Skinner. Despite a late try from academy prop Peter Cook Tigers lost, conceding a further try taking the total to four.

Date: **Friday 28th March 2003**	
Northampton Wanderers	12
Tigers Extras	24

The Extras were out for revenge in this away game against their local rivals - having lost there home fixture earlier in the season. The all-star team included both Austin Healey and all-black legend Josh Kronfeld. Tigers were on the warpath - a strong series of forward drives from the impressive pack resulted in a Gareth Raynor try - converted by Sam Vesty playing at full back. Kronfeld and the man of the match Will Johnson both scored from text book examples of the rolling maul. Raynor rounded off Tigers mauling of the local team which left coach John Wells delighted "Overall that was a very good display against a strong Northampton side. We can take a a lot of positives from tonight"

For up-to-date fixture information, log onto www.leicestertigers.com

Date: **Monday 24th April 2003**	
Tigers Extras	57
Newport	10

Tigers Extras ended their season with a veritable try fest against the young Newport side - an excellent antidote to the bitter pill of the previous day's defeat to Munster. Starting the scoring with a sixth minute try by scrum half Jamie Hamilton. The points continued to add up with the Tigers pack firmly in control. The first half saw tries from Glenn Gelderbloom, Gareth Raynor, Peter Cook - and a second for Jamie Hamilton. At half time the Tigers led 33-5. Despite the already impressive score line the Tigers only let there guard slip for five minutes - Newport sneaking back a try, the rest of the half was every bit as intensive - with a further four tries including a hat-trick for centre Dan Hipkiss.

Tries: Booth, Stimpson, Buckland
Cons: Stimpson (3)

Position	No.	Player
Full Back	15	T.Stimpson
Right Wing	14	G.Raynor
Centre	13	G.Gelderbloom (c)
Centre	12	R.Kafer
Left Wing	11	S.Booth
Fly Half	10	C.McMullen
Scrum Half	9	T.Tierney
Prop	1	P.Freshwater
Hooker	2	G.Chuter
Prop	3	R.Nebbett
Lock	4	P.Short
Lock	5	L.Deacon
Flanker	6	W.Johnson
Flanker	7	L.Abraham
No.8	8	A.Balding

Replacements: J.Buckland, M.Poole, B.Gerry, R.Cooke, J.Wells, D.Richards, N.Jones, S.Vesty, L.Myring, T.Underwood, R.Underwood, A.Key, D.Garforth

They rolled back the years at Welford Road as the Barbarians returned for the first time in five years and some of Tigers former stars pulled on the striped shirt which made them famous.

Both sides tried hard, a bit too hard at times, to entertain the crowd of 6,890 but the spectators didn't worry about that. The whole point of the evening was to pay tribute to the outstanding career of Leicester, England and British Lions Flanker, Neil Back, who had generously offered to make a substantial contribution to the families of PCs Andrew Munn and Bryan Moore who were killed on duty in Leicestershire last Summer.

Tigers legend Richard Cockerill even travelled back from his new home in the South of France to grace a Barbarians side which included such great names as Craig Dowd, Trevor Leota, Jim Williams and Nicki Little. Another former Tigers star Waisale Serevi also brightened up the last few minutes but the biggest roar was reserved for golden oldies Dean Richards, John Wells, Matt Poole and Rory and Tony Underwood.

> "There were many comments from my team mates about whether 24 represented my collar size or my weight. I couldn't even bend over to tie my own shoelaces until Wednesday morning."
> – **Dean Richards**

The first half saw unusually good defence for a Babas fixture with just two scores coming from Norm Berryman and Diego Albanese and a solitary Nicki Little conversion making the half time score 12-0 to the visitors.

Tigers moved up a gear after the break when Steve Booth showed his illustrious opponents a thing or two about quality finishing with a 50 metre solo effort that would have graced any game. Tigers goal machine Tim Stimpson added the extras and then powered his way through for a fine try of his own to take Tigers into a 14-12 lead with two minutes left on the clock.

There was yet another uncontested scrum fiasco

Barbarians

Tries: Berryman, Albanese
Cons: Little

when Richards, Poole, Wells and co attempted to power over from five metres not realising that the front rows had come to the kind of gentleman's agreement you only get in this type of fixture.

The final word went to one of the hosts' promising new generation of talent as hooker James Buckland, Cabbage to his friends, intercepted a wayward pass from scrum half Morgan Williams to trundle in between the sticks from 40 metres. Stimpson added a conversion to send everyone home happy, especially those two deserving families.

Neil Back said afterwards, "I would like to personally thank everybody who made the effort to be here tonight. When I was first asked if I could help this cause I was delighted to say yes with no hesitation. I have met both families tonight, there are five children aged between four and 14, and as a father of two myself, I can't begin to think what they must be feeling. I hope we've managed to help them in some small way tonight."

Position	No.	Player
Full Back	15	T.Delport
Right Wing	14	D.Albanese
Centre	13	S.Bonetti
Centre	12	N.Berryman
Left Wing	11	P.Bonduy
Fly Half	10	N.Little
Scrum Half	9	M.Williams
Prop	1	C.Dowd
Hooker	2	R.Cockerill (c)
Prop	3	D.Morris
Lock	4	B.Cockbain
Lock	5	T.Jacques
Flanker	6	A.Audebert
Flanker	7	W.Brosnihan
No.8	8	J.Williams

Replacements: A.Garvey, S.Miall, V.Satala, W.Serevi, T.Leota, B.Wheeler, M.Denney

Leicester   ✚ Alliance & Leicester

Dean Richards

Position: **Director of Rugby**

D.o.B: **11.07.1963**

Dean was born in Nuneaton, Warwickshire and attended John Cleveland College in Hinckley, before venturing to France to play for Roanne. He joined Tigers and made his debut at Neath in 1982. Within a year he was back in the principality again, this time on tour with the Barbarians.

His England debut followed in March 1986 against Ireland at Twickenham where he became the first player in 57 years to score two tries on an England debut. In 1989 he toured Australia with the British Lions.

Dean has been involved in all Leicester's league title wins, as a player in '88, as captain in '95 and as Director of Rugby in the '98/'99, '99/'00, '00/01 & 01/02 seasons. He is the world's most-capped No. 8.

Andy Key

Backs Coach and Head of Rugby Development

D.o.B: **15.01.1959**

Andy, who is known to all as Kiwi, was born in Market Harborough, educated at Welland Park High School, Market Harborough Grammar School and Leicester Polytechnic.

He played for the Tigers between 1975-81 and again from 1987-92. In between these two periods he played for Bedford and Nottingham. Andy's father, Maurice, played for Tigers in the late '50's while his two brothers, Richard and Lance, have both been professional footballers.

Andy spent 15 years in total at BSS Group Plc before joining Tigers as the full-time General Operations Manager. He has since been appointed as Head of Rugby Development at the club.

John Wells

Position: **Forwards Coach**

D.o.B: **12.05.1963**

John was born in Driffield and attended Magnus Grammar School and Loughborough University, where he studied sports science and recreation management. He has played for Notts, Lincs & Derbys, as well as for Midlands. He represented England U16, U18, Students, U23 and England A as a blind-side flanker. He also played for an England XV against Italy in 1990.

His debut for Tigers was in 1982 at Harlequins and he went on to play for them over 360 times, as captain from '91-'93.

Senior Coaches

Chris Brookes
Position: **Physiotherapist (Rehab Co-ordinator)**

Chris worked as a physiotherapist for Loughborough Students RFC and Syston RFC before joining Tigers in November 2001.

He is a member of the Profile Sports injury risk management team and has worked for the NHS and private clinics for four years.

He is a state registered physiotherapist and has a degree in physiotherapy and is a member of the chartered society of physiotherapy.

John Duggan
Position: **Fitness and Conditioning Coach**
D.o.B: **05.06.1948**

John was born in Dublin and spent his early years travelling the world, especially to the Far East, including Malaya and Singapore. His family eventually settled in Oakham, where he attended Oakham School. He studied physical education and biology at Loughborough College and qualified as a teacher. Before turning his hand to professional rugby, John lectured PE and Fitness next door to the Welford Road ground at Southfields College. He made his Tigers debut in 1970 at Bath and, in a career spanning ten years, he played in 302 games and scored 158 tries. He wanted to play for Ireland but this never transpired since John wasn't playing provincial rugby, which was an Irish requirement at the time.

Dr Dave Finlay
Position: **Team Doctor**
D.o.B: **06.02.1947**

Originally from Grimsby, Dr Finlay qualified in medicine at St Andrews University in 1970. He worked in orthopaedics, trauma, casualty and medicine before becoming a radiologist in 1977. He was made a consultant at Queens Medical Centre in Nottingham in 1978 and moved to his current job at Leicester Royal Infirmary in 1981 as Muscular Skeletal Radiologist.

The Doc has been involved with Tigers since 1982 when he worked alongside fellow doctor Mike Allen. He has been first team doctor for over a decade.

Senior Coaches

Mark Geeson

Position: **Physiotherapist**

D.o.B: **03.01.1959**

Mark was educated at Oadby Beauchamp College and at the University Hospital of Wales where he became a chartered physiotherapist.

He joined Tigers in 1993, after working as physio for Kettering Town FC, Grimsby Town FC and Leicester City FC (1989-92).

Mark has also been the physio for the England Under-21 football team and Leicester Panthers American Football team.

Damian McGrath

Position: **Skills Coach**

Damian played for Swinton RLFC and Batley RLFC before coaching for Leeds Rhinos and London Broncos in the Super League. He was also the assistant coach for the England Rugby League World Cup squad in 2000.

After coaching the Great Britain U19s rugby league squad, Damian switched codes and joined rugby union as the defence coach for England 'A' in 2002. In the same year he was England 7s skills and defence coach before joining Tigers in July 2002.

Damian has also worked as a school teacher and a Rugby League Development Officer.

Cliff Shephard

Position: **Team Secretary**

D.o.B: **21.02.1935**

Cliff was born in Wigston and educated at Wigston HS. He played as a wing in the Leicester Schools' team and in a final England Schools' trial. He captained the Leicestershire Alliance Colts and represented the county and RAF.

His Tigers debut was in 1955 against Coventry, and he went on to play for the Tigers First XV 140 times, scoring 36 tries. Cliff became the LFC first team secretary in 1996 after looking after the Extras in the same capacity for a few years. Before his retirement, Cliff was a sales representative with Bass Breweries.

Martin Johnson Position: **Lock**

D.o.B: **9.3.70**
P.o.B: **Solihull**
Height: **6' 6"**
Weight: **18st 12lb**

Tigers Debut: **14.2.89 v RAF**
Tigers Record: **301+10 apps, 75 pts**
Previous Clubs: **Wigston, College OB (NZ), King Country (NZ)**
Rep Hons: **England (76), British Lions (8), Barbarians**

Tigers' captain Martin Johnson holds a unique position in world rugby as the only man ever to captain the British Lions on two separate tours, to South Africa in 1997 and Australia in 2001. To add to that achievement Martin captained the England team to their Grand Slam victory in the 2002-3 Six Nations Championship, their first Grand Slam since 1995, and their first in the expanded competition. Martin's international career began when he played for the England 18-Group in 1987. He joined Tigers' senior squad in 1989, and in the summer of that year played for King Country in New Zealand and was selected for the NZ U21 tour to Australia the following year. In 1990, he made his Midlands debut, and in '92 was selected for England B and the Barbarians. Martin made his England debut as a last minute replacement for Wade Dooley in '93, and went on later that year to play numerous England A internationals and toured NZ with the British Lions. He has been involved in all 10 Five/Six Nations tournaments since his debut (1994-2003) and 3 Lions Tours (NZ '93, SA '97 and AUS '01). Martin played in the World Cups in 1995 and in '99, taking the captaincy in '99, and has gone on to break Dooley's record as England's most capped lock. He first captained England in 1998 and by the 2002-03 Grand slam decider had led his country on 30 occasions; England have lost only one of their last 19 games with him in charge. He was named the 1998-99 Allied Dunbar Premiership Player of the Season and since being appointed Tigers' club captain in '97 has led the Leicester team to four successive Premiership victories between 1999-2002, as well as the inaugural Zurich Championship title and European Heineken Cup in successive seasons, 2001 and 2002. Martin, regarded as a stalwart at lock, is also Leicester's longest ever serving captain and in the home game against Bristol in February 2003, became the 33rd player to have made 300 appearances for the club.

Player Profiles

Luke Abraham
Position: **Back Row**

Tigers Debut: **21.12.02 v Worcester Warriors**
Tigers Record: **0+2 apps**
Rep Hons: **England U21A**

Luke joined the Tigers Academy at the age of 15, only three years after he took up the sport at Bushlow High School and joined his local club, Leicester Vipers. Since then he has worked his way through the Youth team and was part of the Tigers' successful U21 squad that claimed the 2002/3 League title. Luke was selected for the England U18 Schoolboys squad to face New Zealand Schoolboys at Twickenham at the end of January 2001, and then elevated to the U19 team, playing against Ireland and France in their shadow Six Nations. He played in the FIRA U19 Junior World Championship in Italy in March 2002 and more recently has represented England U21A.

D.o.B: **26.9.83**
P.o.B: **Leicester**
Height: **6' 2"**
Weight: **16st, 5lb**

Neil Back
Position: **Openside Flanker**

Tigers Debut: **1.9.90 v Bedford**
Tigers Record: **274+16 apps, 530 pts**
Previous Clubs: **Barker's Butts, Nottingham**
Rep Hons: **England (59), British Lions (4), Barbarians**

A mark of the esteem in which Neil Back is held was shown when the Barbarians accepted an invitation to play a Leicester XV as part of Neil's testimonial season, a rare honour for an individual player. For England he has been involved in two World Cups ('95, '99) as well as six Five/Six Nations campaigns (1998-2003), captaining his country on four occasions. He was in the England squad to tour New Zealand and Australia in summer 2003. Neil represented England at U18, U21 and England A level before making his full England debut against Scotland in 1994. He has played regularly for the Barbarians. In 1998 he was named RFU "Player of the Year", and in 1999 the Professional Rugby Players Association's " Players' Player of the Year" when he was also the league's top try scorer with 16! 'Backy' holds the Club's career league try-scoring record (64 at the end of season 2002-03). Recipient of the supporters' Outstanding Service Award for season 2002/3, Neil is also just 10 appearances short of joining the '300 Club'.

D.o.B: **16.1.69**
P.o.B: **Coventry**
Height: **5' 10"**
Weight: **14st 8lb**

Adam Balding Position: No. 8

Tigers Debut: **29.11.98 at Rugby Lions**
Tigers Record: **39+54 apps, 20 pts**
Previous Clubs: **Broadstreet, Coventry**
Rep Hons: **England A**

Since making his debut for Tigers in 1998 Adam has shown immense talent; his much admired ability resulted in the award of the 1999-2000 Tigers' Young Player of the Season. He has represented England at U16, U18 and U21 level and during the 2001-02 season played for England A against Wales A in the 'shadow' Six Nations tournament. He was selected for the England 7s squad for the World 7s Series in Chile and Argentina in January 2002. He was later chosen for the England party to tour Argentina in the summer of 2002, playing for the England XV against Argentina A and then chosen on the bench for the full international. He was also named in the original extended England squad prior to their game with the Barbarians in the summer of 2003. Before concentrating on rugby, Adam played cricket and used to swim for his school, Caludon Castle. He joined his first club, Coventry Saracens, at the age of six and eventually came to Welford Road under a scholarship scheme along with former teammates Andy Goode and James Grindal.

D.o.B: **7.12.79**
P.o.B: **Coventry**
Height: **6' 2"**
Weight: **17st**

Steve Booth Position: Wing / Full Back

Tigers Debut: **6.9.00 v Rotherham**
Tigers Record: **45+18 apps, 173 pts**
Previous Clubs: **Oulton ARL, Huddersfield Giants RL, Doncaster Dragons RL**
Rep Hons: **England 7s**

Steve joined Tigers in August 2000, scoring a try on his debut against Rotherham. He ended the 2001-02 season as Tigers' joint top Premiership try scorer along with Geordan Murphy, with nine tries apiece, and in 2002-03 was the sole top try scorer with 10 touchdowns in all competitions. His kick in the 21-11 victory over Northampton Saints at Franklin's Gardens in October 2001 saw him become the first Tigers winger to drop a goal in a match since Bob Barker in February '76. Steve is considered a threat by defenders because of his pace and ability to get through tackles, a trait that was acknowledged when he was named the Zurich Player of the Month in January 2002. His ability was rewarded when he was called into the England 7s squad and played twice for England A in the 'shadow' Six Nations tournament 2001/2. However, he missed out on the full England tour to Argentina in the summer of 2002 due to injury.

D.o.B: **18.9.76**
P.o.B: **Pontefract**
Height: **5' 8"**
Weight: **12st 5lb**

Player Profiles

Ross Broadfoot Position: **Fly Half**

Previous Clubs: **Saracens, London Irish**
Rep Hons: **England 16 Group Schools,
18 Group Schools (September 1), Under-19**

Fly-half Ross Broadfoot is seen as a great prospect for the future. The left footed place kicker has already represented England at 16 Group Schools in 1999/2000 and 2000/01, 18 Group Schools (1 September) 2001/02 and Under 19s 2002/03. He played three games for England Under 19s in the FIRA World Championship in France this season including the 5th/6th place decider against Ireland that went to a penalty shoot out after ending in a 22 all draw, scoring a conversion, drop goal and four penalties during the game. A pupil at Whitgift School, Croydon, Ross was a member of their squad that won the Daily Mail Under 15 Cup in 1999. He plays cricket as a hobby.

D.o.B: **8.3.85**
P.o.B: **Lewisham**
Height: **5' 11"**
Weight: **13st**

James Buckland Position: **Hooker**

Previous Clubs: **Aylesbury RFC, Northampton**
Rep Hons: **England U21**

James joined the Tigers in the summer of 2002 from Northampton Saints, where he had been playing for the previous four years. He had just returned from South Africa where he had travelled with England for the U21 IRB World Championship tournament. Although coming from a boxing background, James chose rugby, and joined his local club Aylesbury RFC. It was after a trip with them to Northampton that he was offered the chance to join the Saints. He made his first appearance in Tigers' stripes in the Middlesex 7s tournament at Twickenham in August 2002 and then joined the first team at their training camp in France, playing in the friendly match against Agen. He was a regular member of Tigers' league winning U21 team last season, his 12 tries making him the U21's top try scorer. He was also on the bench for Tigers' home game against his former club, Northampton, in November.

D.o.B: **21.9.81**
P.o.B: **Aylesbury**
Height: **5' 11"**
Weight: **16st 9lb**

Player Profiles

George Chuter Position: **Hooker**

Tigers Debut: **31.3.01 v Gloucester**
Tigers Record: **15+24 apps, 10 pts**
Previous Clubs: **Old Mid-Whitgiftians, Saracens**
Rep Hons: **England A**

Having previously played for Saracens, with whom he won the Cup in '98, George joined Tigers in December 2000, and after the departure of Richard Cockerill in the summer of 2002, vied with Dorian West as first choice at hooker. After playing for London Division at both U18 and U21 level George was invited to trial for Saracens. He joined their first team squad at the age of 19 and had five years with them before taking a break from rugby to travel, visiting Australia and the USA. He made his England A debut in 1998 scoring a try in the game against France at Tours, and went on to be included in the summer '98 tour to Australia and New Zealand, featuring in the match at Invercargill against New Zealand Academies. An old boy of Trinity School in Croydon, George played club rugby for Old Mid-Whitgiftians before studying at the West London Institute for a year.

D.o.B: **9.7.76**
P.o.B: **Greenwich**
Height: **5' 10'**
Weight: **16st 4lb**

Peter Cook Position: **Prop**

Tigers Debut: **19.4.03 at NEC Harlequins**
Tigers Record: **1 app**
Rep Hons: **England U21**

On his Tigers' debut against Harlequins, when he faced England's 100 cap stalwart Jason Leonard in the front row, Peter Cook became the 15th Academy player since its inception to start for the Tigers' first XV. A member of Leicester's successful 2002/3 U21 squad, Peter also represented England U21 during the Six Nations and was included in the 2003 England U21 World Cup squad having previously been capped at U18 Schools level. A Coventry lad, Cook followed footsteps Adam Balding and played for the Broadstreet club when he was six, he came to the Tigers aged 16 after writing to the club and being offered trial.

D.o.B: **25.12.82**
P.o.B: **Coventry**
Height: **5' 10"**
Weight: **16st 1lb**

Player Profiles

Martin Corry
Position: **Back Row / Lock**

Tigers Debut: **30.8.97 v Gloucester**
Tigers Record: **156+9 apps, 80 pts**
Previous Clubs: **Newcastle-Gosforth, Bristol**
Rep Hons: **England (25), British Lions (3), Barbarians**

Originally overlooked by the 2001 British Lions, Martin was called in as a late replacement and was in great form, eventually playing in all three tests. After playing in the delayed Six Nations decider in Dublin in October 2001 Martin missed out on the Autumn internationals but was a bench replacement for the 2002 Six Nations. He played four games for England A last season including one as captain in Ireland, and was included in Clive Woodward's squad to tour New Zealand and Australia in the summer of 2003. Having started playing rugby in the mini section at Tunbridge Wells RFC, Martin first represented England at U18 level in 1992 in the team that won the junior grand slam and triple crown. He was included in the England Students side in 1995 and later that year, England A. Martin made his England Test debut in 1997 in Argentina, and since joining Tigers in '97, he has played for his country in four Five/Six Nations tournaments (1998-2002) and featured in the 1999 World Cup. He was named as the Members' Player of the Season in 1999-2000.

D.o.B: **12.10.73**
P.o.B: **Birmingham**
Height: **6' 5"**
Weight: **17st 5lb**

Brett Deacon
Position: **Flanker**

Rep Hons: **England U19**

Brett started playing rugby at the age of seven for Wigston RFC, and went to South Wigston High School. He moved to Syston when he was 11 and went on to represent the County, Midlands and England at U16 and U18 levels. He was selected for the England U19 squad for the shadow Six Nations 2001/2, and in fact captained them in their game against Wales U19 in January this year. At school he enjoyed playing football and basketball, but now concentrates solely on rugby. Brett, who is the younger brother of Tigers lock, Louis, joined the Tigers, Youth Team at the age of 15, and has played for the U21 team. He is one of three Tigers, Academy players who took part in training programme at the South African Institute of Rugby in Durban, South Africa, in the summer of 2001.

D.o.B: **7.3.82**
P.o.B: **Leicester**
Height: **6' 3"**
Weight: **17st**

Player Profiles

Louis Deacon Position: **Lock**

Tigers Debut: **12.8.00 v Cardiff**
Tigers Record: **49+8 apps, 10 pts**
Previous Clubs: **Wigston, Syston**
Rep Hons: **England U21**

Since making his Tigers first team debut as a replacement against Cardiff in August 2000, Louis has established himself as a highly dependable player in the Tigers first XV at either front or middle jumper. A former pupil of Ratcliffe College Leicester, Louis started playing rugby as an eight-year-old with Wigston. He later joined Syston and proceeded to play for the County, the Midlands and England at U16 level. Since joining the Tigers Academy in 1997-98 he has appeared in the Tigers' Youth, U21 and Extras teams. He has also progressed to England U18 and U21 rugby and was called into the England A squad last season, but injury denied him the chance of playing.

D.o.B: **7.10.80**
P.o.B: **Leicestershire**
Height: **6' 6"**
Weight: **17st 12lb**

Harry Ellis Position: **Scrum Half**

Tigers Debut: **25.8.01 at Stade Toulousain**
Tigers Record: **31+19 apps, 35 pts**
Previous Clubs: **South Leicester, Wigston**
Rep Hons: **England U21**

Harry started playing rugby as a 6-year-old with South Leicester, before moving to Wigston for a year and joining Tigers' Youth Team in 1997. The youngest of three rugby-playing brothers, Harry studied at Leicester Grammar School and had previously represented Leicestershire Schools at 14, 16 and 18 year age groups, before going on to compete for the Midlands at U16 and U18 level. More notably Harry represented England 'A' at U16, U18, U19 and U21 levels, having appeared in the U18 group whilst only 16, two years younger than most of his teammates. He was one of five Tigers' players included in the 2003 IRB U21 World Cup squad this summer. He also featured for England in the World 7s Series and was invited to attend one of Clive Woodward's England training sessions during 2001-02. Having made his senior debut in the Orange Cup game in Toulouse in August 2001, Harry went on to score a great try that helped defeat Llanelli in the Heineken Cup semi-final at Nottingham in that season. He was the Tigers' Players' Young Player of the Year 2001-02.

D.o.B: **17.5.82**
P.o.B: **Leicester**
Height: **5' 10"**
Weight: **13st 5lb**

Player Profiles

Glenn Gelderbloom Position: **Centre**

Tigers Debut: **12.8.00 at Cardiff**
Tigers Record: **30+33 apps, 15pts**
Previous Clubs: **Western Province, Border Bulldogs, Old Crescent (Ireland)**
Rep Hons: **SA Defence Force, Rest of South Africa**

South African Glenn was educated at Pinelands High School in Cape Town. In 1991-92 he played for Western Province before moving to Border Bulldogs in 1993, where he made over 100 appearances, captaining them in '98 and '99. Glenn joined Tigers in August 2000 after playing in the Irish second division the previous year. As the seasons progressed he became much admired and has since been used as an impact player, bringing his experience to bear on a game. Glenn used to teach Physical Education and History at schools in SA; an all round sportsman, he played cricket at school and club level, and enjoys golf.

D.o.B: **11.12.69**
P.o.B: **Cape Town, SA**
Height: **5' 11"**
Weight: **14st 3lb**

Daryl Gibson Position: **Centre**

Previous Clubs: **Canterbury NPC, Crusaders, Bristol Shoguns**
Rep Hons: **New Zealand (19), New Zealand Maori, Barbarians**

Inside centre Daryl Gibson gained 19 New Zealand caps between his debut against Samoa in Albany in June 1999 and his most recent appearance versus South Africa in the Tri-Nations in August 2002. He played throughout the 1999 Rugby World Cup, his only try for the All Blacks coming against Italy at Huddersfield in that competition. He also appeared in all five games for the New Zealand Maori on their 1998 tour of Scotland. Daryl made a team record 78 appearances for the Crusaders in Super-12 rugby from 1996-2002, gaining three winners medals in 1998, 1999 and 2002. He played 80 matches for Canterbury following his debut in June 1993, claiming 35 tries and winning the New Zealand Provincial Championship with them in 1997 and 2001. Gibson played for New Zealand U19 in 1993 and 1994, and New Zealand U21 in 1994, 1995 and 1996. He joined Bristol Shoguns in September 2002, making his home debut against Leicester Tigers in the Zurich Premiership on 29th September.

D.o.B: **2.3.75**
P.o.B: **Lumsden, NZ**
Height: **5' 11"**
Weight: **15st 3lb**

Player Profiles

James Hamilton Position: **Lock**

Previous Clubs: **Barker's Butts**
Rep Hons: **England U21**

James went to Coundon Court School in Coventry and started playing rugby at the age of 15. He also enjoyed swimming and football, but it was rugby he concentrated on, going to play for well-known club Barker's Butts, the club that launched the careers of Neil Back and Leon Lloyd. James was selected for the England U19 team that took part in the U19 World Cup in Chile, 2000/01, having already played against Wales and France at that level. In 2001/02 he represented England U21 in the shadow Six Nations. He joined the Tigers academy at the end of 1999 and played regularly for Tigers Youth before progressing to Tigers Extras where his good form meant that he was selected on the bench for the Zurich Premiership game at Leeds Tykes in November 2001. James is one of three Tigers' academy players who took part in the training programme in Durban, South Africa in summer 2001.

D.o.B: **17/11/1982**
P.o.B: **Swindon**
Height: **6' 8"**
Weight: **19st 4lb**

Austin Healey Position: **Utility Back**

Tigers Debut: **26.8.96 v Agen**
Tigers Record: **154+14 apps, 246 pts**
Previous Clubs: **Birkenhead Park, Waterloo, Orrell**
Rep Hons: **England (50), British Lions (2), Barbarians**

Austin was hailed as the player who created the break that ended in the winning score in the Heineken Cup final 2001, then scored the second and decisive try against Munster when Tigers retained the cup the following year. A player of pace and unpredictability, Austin's excellent form for Tigers during the 2001 season was rewarded with his inclusion in England's starting line-up during the Six Nations, and selection for the British Lions squad to tour Australia, his second Lions tour, where he put in some stunning match winning performances but unfortunately missed out on further caps due to injury. On his return from 'Down Under' he played in every game for England until he was rested for the summer 2002 tour to Argentina, showing his versatility by starting at full back, scrum half, and on the wing as well as coming on as a replacement twice. He also appeared as a replacement in all three of last season's Autumn internationals when England recorded a hat-trick of victories over their Tri-Nations visitors.

D.o.B: **26.10.73**
P.o.B: **Wallasey**
Height: **5' 10"**
Weight: **14st 4lb**

Player Profiles

Dan Hipkiss Position: **Centre**

Tigers Debut: **24.8.02 at Bayonne v Biarritz**
Tigers Record: **2+1 apps, 5pts**
Rep Hons: **England U21**

Having learnt his trade at Hartsmere School and Diss Rugby Club in Ipswich, Leicester offered Dan a scholarship to Uppingham School and the chance to become involved in the Tigers' Youth set up. Following in his father's footsteps (he played for England Schools), Dan represented England at U16, U17, U18 and U21 levels. He suffered a career threatening injury to his left knee in November 1999, eventually diagnosed as being damage to the cruciate ligament, and was advised never to play again. However, after two years, three operations and plenty of hard work, Dan made his first start for Tigers U21 against Leeds on November 9th 2001, scoring a try on his debut. He was called into the first team squad for summer training in 2002, and scored a stunning solo try on his senior debut in the Orange Cup game against Biarritz in Bayonne. His good performance led to a call up for the opening Zurich Premiership game of the season against Leeds Tykes. Dan was also a regular member of the successful Tigers 2002-03 U21 team and was one of five Tigers called up for the 2003 IRB U21 World Cup.

D.o.B: **4.6.82**
P.o.B: **Ipswich**
Height: **5' 10"**
Weight: **14st 3lb**

Michael Holford Position: **Tighthead Prop**

Previous Clubs: **Syston**
Rep Hons: **England U21**

Born in Leicester, Michael attended Oakham School, gaining a sports scholarship to study for his A-Levels in Sports Science and Biology. He started playing rugby at the age of 10 and has since played for the England U18 Schools' team, England U19s, and was one of three young Tigers' players to represent England in the IRB U21 World Championship in South Africa in the summer of 2002. He was also named in the squad for the IRB World Cup in June 2003. He joined Tigers' Youth set up in 1998 and has played in the Tigers' U21 and Extras teams. A talented young player, Michael has been included in the Tigers last three pre-season training camps in Ulster and France where he played in the training game against Perpignan in the summer of 2001.

D.o.B: **11.8.82**
P.o.B: **Leicester**
Height: **5' 11"**
Weight: **16st 7lb**

Player Profiles

John Holtby Position: **Wing**

D.o.B: **27.3.82**
P.o.B: **Beverley**
Height: **6' 3"**
Weight: **15st 8lb**

Tigers Debut: **20.10.01 v Saracens**
Tigers Record: **6+2 apps, 5pts**
Previous Clubs: **Beverley, Hull Ionians**
Rep Hons: **England U21**

John attended Hull Grammar School, and started playing rugby at the age of 10 for his hometown club in Beverley, East Yorkshire before moving on to Hull Ionians. While at school, he enjoyed taking part in athletics, competing in the decathlon, and playing football. His rugby honours include England U18 Clubs and England U19, and he was selected for the Midlands U21 squad in October 2001 and England U21 for the 'shadow' Six Nations last season. John joined the Tigers' Academy after being spotted by Tigers coach Ian Smith when a student at Loughborough University, where he studied Engineering and Sports Technology. His start to the 2002-03 season was hampered after he suffered a severe shoulder injury in the Orange Cup against Biarritz, but he has recuperated well and returned to score his debut try in the Premiership home game against London Irish.

Will Johnson Position: **Back Row**

D.o.B: **18.3.74**
P.o.B: **Solihull**
Height: **6' 4"**
Weight: **17st**

Tigers Debut: **16.4.94 at Sale**
Tigers Record: **106+32 apps, 35 pts**
Previous Clubs: **Wigston, Kibworth, Linwood (NZ)**
Rep Hons: **England A**

The 2002-03 season saw Will Johnson consolidate his position in the Tigers' back row, despite some stiff opposition. He has now started alongside his brother Martin in 51 Tigers teams. Educated at Robert Smyth School in Market Harborough, then at Birmingham University, before making his Tigers debut in 1994, Will played Midlands 18, 19 and 21 Group rugby. His 1999-2000 season was cut short when he fractured his foot in the first week of April, however sparkling form in the 2000-01 season resulted in Will being picked as vice-captain of England A during the 2001 'shadow' Six Nations, after having scored a try on his debut in the 44-3 victory over Italy A at Bedford in February 2001. Despite this, he unfortunately missed out on the full tour to Canada in the summer of that year, but came back into contention for the England A squad, most recently turning out for them against Wales in March 2002.

Player Profiles

Ben Kay Position: **Lock**

Tigers Debut: **11.9.99 at Northampton**
Tigers Record: **98+18 apps, 35 pts**
Previous Clubs: **Waterloo, Queensland University (Aus)**
Rep Hons: **England (21), Barbarians**

Ben was educated at Merchant Taylor's School before attending Loughborough University. He has played rugby at Queensland University in Australia, and represented England U18, U19, Students and U21 and appeared for the Barbarians in '99. Joining Tigers from Waterloo in 1999, Ben made his England A debut against France in 2000, going on to captain the A team in 2001. He was in fine form for Tigers in the 2000-01 season and as a result was chosen for England to tour Canada and the USA. Ben was in the starting line-up for all the Six Nations games in spring 2002, and scored a try against Ireland. After another outstanding season he was named as the Members Player of the Year 2001-02 and was nominated for the Zurich Premiership Player of the Year. After touring Argentina with England in the summer of 2002, Ben competed in both the Autumn internationals and the Six Nations. He has played in every England game since November 2001 and has been on the losing side just once in his 19 international caps, against France in March 2002.

D.o.B: **14.12.75**
P.o.B: **Liverpool**
Height: **6' 6"**
Weight: **18st 3lb**

Josh Kronfeld Position: **Flanker**

Tigers Debut: **25.8.01 at Stade Toulousain**
Tigers Record: **36+10 apps, 45 pts**
Previous Clubs: **Otago NPC, Highlanders**
Rep Hons: **New Zealand (54) Barbarians**

Flanker Josh Kronfeld is one of New Zealand's most experienced players. Josh played his early rugby at scrum half and centre, switching to flanker at high school. He made his senior debut for an Otago XV in 1992. He has played Super-12 rugby for the Otago Highlanders for five seasons. Between 1998 and 2000 Josh played 36 out of a possible 37 Super-12 games and was a losing finalist against Canterbury in 1999. He played in the 1995 Rugby World Cup, including the final in which the All Blacks lost a thrilling game to South Africa. Kronfeld joined Tigers as New Zealand's most capped flanker of all time and became the first All Black since Ernest Booth (in 1909) to play for the club. An injury-hit start to the 2001-02 season saw Josh recover well, establishing himself as a regular first team player and a crowd favourite. He confirmed that position last season after some outstanding performances, twice being voted by fans as Player of the Month and then named by his Tigers' colleagues as their Players' Player of the Season 2002-03.

D.o.B: **20.6.71**
P.o.B: **Hastings, NZ**
Height: **6' 1"**
Weight: **15st 11lb**

Player Profiles

Leon Lloyd Position: **Wing / Centre**

Tigers Debut: **16.10.96 at Leinster**
Tigers Record: **160+15 apps, 295 pts**
Previous Clubs: **Barker's Butts**
Rep Hons: **England (5), Barbarians**

Prior to making his debut for the Tigers first team Leon was a successful try scorer for the Tigers Youth XV and Development XV before a serious car accident sidelined him for six months. He made his full Tigers debut in 1996 and was part of the squad that won the Madrid 7s that year. He scored his first memorable try in the Heineken Cup victory at Pau. Leon was selected for England Colts, the Barbarians and England U21 in 1997, two years later he played for England A, and also equalled Rory Underwood's 1985 Club record of four tries scored in a single Cup tie. Leon's England debut came against South Africa in the summer of 2000, and he appeared again on their tour to Canada and the USA in 2001. Unfortunately, he suffered a shoulder injury which required surgery and kept him out of the Tigers squad for the start of the 2001-02 season. However, Leon recovered well only to be cruelly struck down by injury again. After a delayed start to the 2002-03 season Leon played in 27 of a possible 29 matches following his return against Bath in October.

D.o.B: **22.9.77**
P.o.B: **Coventry**
Height: **6' 4"**
Weight: **14st 12lb**

Lewis Moody Position: **Flanker**

Tigers Debut: **25.08.96 v Boroughmuir**
Tigers Record: **94+37 apps, 90 pts**
Previous Clubs: **Oakham, Bracknell**
Rep Hons: **England (14)**

All-round sportsman Lewis competed in athletics, cricket and swimming at school before deciding to concentrate on rugby. He first played for the Tigers in the youth team in 1995, and scored two tries on his first team debut in '96. He has also played for England Schools, U18, Colts and England U21, and in '98 was selected for the full England tour to the southern hemisphere where he featured in games against NZ Academy and NZ Maoris. After a superb season for Tigers, he was finally awarded his full international cap on the England tour to Canada and the USA in 2001. Continued impressive form saw him challenge his teammate, Neil Back, for the coveted England No.7 shirt, starting in two Six Nations games the following season. 2002-03 saw him play in all three of the Autumn internationals, scoring a try in the game against New Zealand, but unfortunately he was injured in the last game against South Africa. Lewis was named Zurich Player of the Month for September 2001, and the 2001-02 Zurich Young Player of the Season.

D.o.B: **12.6.78**
P.o.B: **Ascot**
Height: **6' 4"**
Weight: **16st 6lb**

Player Profiles

Darren Morris Position: **Prop**

Previous Clubs: **Neath, Swansea**
Rep Hons: **Wales (15), British Lions (1), Barbarians**

Educated at Aberdare Boys Comprehensive, Neath College and Glamorgan University, Darren Morris originally came to prominence with Neath before joining Swansea in 1998. In his time with the 'All-Whites' they lifted the Welsh Cup in 1999 with a 37-10 win over Llanelli at Cardiff's Ninian Park, and he was also part of the squad that won the Welsh-Scottish League in 2000-01. Darren was included in the Swansea team that lost to Leicester in the Heineken Cup quarter-final tie at Welford Road in January 2001. Morris has won 15 Wales caps since his debut against Zimbabwe in Harare in June 1998, scoring one try against Argentina at the Millennium Stadium in November 2001. He also toured Australia with the British & Irish Lions in 2001 playing in six matches, including coming on as a replacement in the 3rd test in Sydney. Darren has appeared twice for the Barbarians – against Australia at the Millennium Stadium in November 2001 and the East Midlands in the Mobbs Memorial Match at Northampton the following May.

D.o.B: **24.9.74**
P.o.B: **Pontypridd**
Height: **6' 1"**
Weight: **18st 12lb**

Geordan Murphy Position: **Full Back / Wing**

Tigers Debut: **14.11.97 v Rotherham**
Tigers Record: **117+13 apps, 468 pts**
Previous Clubs: **Naas (Ireland), Auckland GS (NZ)**
Rep Hons: **Ireland (17), Barbarians**

Born in Dublin, the youngest of six children who all played rugby union, Geordan attended De Montfort University in Leicester. Shortly after joining Tigers in 1997, he gained his first cap for his country playing at U18 level. In '98 Geordan was the Tigers Extras' top try scorer with 10 tries, and had scored the most points at 128. In June 2000, he made his full Ireland debut against the United States, scoring twice. Top form in the 2000-01 season saw him turning out regularly for Ireland A during the 'shadow' Six Nations and led to him being picked for the Barbarians tour of the UK and Ireland in 2001. That season he also finished as Tigers top try scorer in all competitions. He toured with Ireland in the summer of 2002, adding two more caps to his tally, but missed the start of Tigers 2002-03 campaign after undergoing surgery. He returned to fitness in time to participate in the Autumn internationals, and was ever-present for his country in the 2003 Six Nations. Geordan was voted Members Player of the Season for 2002/03.

D.o.B: **19.4.78**
P.o.B: **Dublin**
Height: **6' 1"**
Weight: **13st 3lb**

Player Profiles

Ricky Nebbett Position: **Prop**

Tigers Debut: **7.4.00 v Munster**
Tigers Record: **25+30 apps**
Previous Clubs: **Harlequins**
Rep Hons: **England Tourist**

Ricky started playing rugby as a seven year old after seeing a poster for local club Sutton & Epsom at his school. He was originally tried out on the wing, moved to flanker, but found his best position at prop. After an eight year career at Quins, who he joined as a 15-year-old, Ricky came to the Tigers in March 2000. Since then he has played for England U-21s, was selected for England A during the 2000-01 'shadow' Six Nations, and was also included in the England squad to tour Canada and the USA in 2001. Unfortunately, he did not gain a cap. A continuation of his good form saw him start three games in the 2001-02 'shadow' competition whilst last season he was called into the senior England training squad.

D.o.B: **16.8.77**
P.o.B: Kingston-upon-Thames
Height: **5' 10"**
Weight: **17st 5lb**

Ramiro Pez Position: **Fly Half**

Previous Clubs: **La Tablada (Arg), Rugby Roma (It), Rotherham**
Rep Hons: **Italy (14)**

Argentine born Ramiro Pez played for La Tablada in his home town of Cordoba and was fly-half when they won the Argentinian club title for the only time in November 2000, scoring all 23 points in a 23-22 victory over Duendes Rosario. In March 2000 he joined Rugby Roma in Italy scoring 122 points and six tries in 19 Serie A appearances over the next season and a half including an Italian Championship final win over L'Aquila in Rome in June 2000 where he scored 20 points himself before being forced off at half-time due to injury. Pez has gained 14 Italian caps since his debut in July 2000 against Samoa in Apia where he scored nine points. A left-footed kicker, he has now has accumulated 70 international points scoring three tries for Italy including two in his last two tests against France and Scotland in this year's Six Nations Tournament. He joined Rotherham in 2001-02, guiding them to the National Division One title as their top points scorer with 202 points and repeated the feat this season, this time with 264 points breaking Mike Umaga's previous Rotherham record of points in a league season.

D.o.B: **6.12.78**
P.o.B: **Cordoba, Arg**
Height: **5' 9"**
Weight: **13st 5lb**

Player Profiles

Graham Rowntree Position: **Prop**

Tigers Debut: **23.10.90 v Oxford University**
Tigers Record: **299+31 apps, 82 pts**
Previous Clubs: **Nuneaton Colts**
Rep Hons: **England (44), Barbarians**

Since joining Tigers Youth in 1988, Graham has gone on to make over 300 appearances for the Tigers, the 32nd player in the club's history to reach that milestone. Graham is also only the third player in Tigers history, after Darren Garforth and Martin Johnson, to play in 150 league games, and in the 1999-00 season he won the award for Outstanding Service to the Club. In '93 he made his England A, Barbarians and Midlands debuts, and in 1995 he gained his first full England cap against Scotland in the Five Nations tournament. He was a prominent figure in the next two Five Nations tournaments, the '95 and '99 World Cups, and also in the Lions Tour to South Africa in '97, playing six games. After the World Cup Graham was not capped for almost two years until a series of imperious performances for the club forced him back into international contention. He missed out on the Summer 2002 tour to Argentina, and was injured for the Autumn internationals, but his club form ensured that he was an ever-present in the 2003 Six Nations Championship.

D.o.B: **18.4.71**
P.o.B: **Stockton-on-Tees**
Height: **6' 0"**
Weight: **16st 7lb**

Will Skinner Position: **Flanker**

Tigers Debut: **26.4.03 v Leeds Tykes**
Tigers Record: **2+3 apps, 5 pts**
Previous Clubs: **Olney, Bedford**
Rep Hons: **England 7s**

Will began playing rugby when, at the age of six, he followed in the footsteps of his two older brothers and joined Olney Rugby Club, he then moved to Bedford RFC at U13 level. After earning three caps for England Schoolboys at U16 level, he was invited to join the Tigers' Academy as a 16 year old by Tigers' head of rugby development, And Key. The openside flanker has continued to improve and was picked for the England U18 squad that played at Welford Road at the end of February 2001. Whilst still waiting to make his impressive Tigers first team debut, he played in the England 7s team that won the Brisbane 7s in Feb 2003 and for England U19s during the Six Nations. He was also called into the England U21 training squad for their game against Scotland.

D.o.B: **8.2.84**
P.o.B: **Northampton**
Height: **5' 11"**
Weight: **14st 2lb**

Ollie Smith Position: Centre

Tigers Debut: **16.9.00 v London Irish**
Tigers Record: **52+11 apps, 85 pts**
Previous Clubs: **Old Bosworthians, Market Bosworth**
Rep Hons: **England (1)**

Since making his first team debut in September 2000, Ollie has been a regular in the starting line-up. He was the 2000-01 and 2001-02 Members' Young Player of the Season, as well as the Vauxhall Young Player of the Season in 2000-01. He has surpassed Lewis Moody's record as the youngest Tigers player to play in a league game. He played for England U18 'A' in 1999-2000 and the next season became a member of the England U19 team, progressing to the U21 side during 2001-02. He made his senior debut as a replacement in the Six Nations game against Italy at Twickenham in March. His performance during a season curtailed by injury earned him a nomination for Young Player of the Season 2002-03 by the Professional Rugby Players Association. Ollie has also appeared as an uncapped player for the Barbarians, in their game against Wales at the Millennium Stadium in Cardiff in 2002, his second appearance at the venue after helping Tigers win the Heineken Cup there a few days earlier. He is the only teenager to hold a Heineken Cup winners medal.

D.o.B: **14.8.82**
P.o.B: **Leicester**
Height: **6' 1"**
Weight: **15st**

Tim Stimpson Position: Full Back / Wing

Tigers Debut: **5.9.98 v Harlequins**
Tigers Record: **136+9 apps, 1653 pts**
Previous Clubs: **Wakefield, West Hartlepool, Newcastle Falcons**
Rep Hons: **England (19), British Lions (1), Barbarians**

Tim Stimpson ended the 2002-03 season as Tigers' top points scorer, a position claimed for the fourth consecutive year. His 12 points in the home game against Northampton on 30 November 2002 saw him become only the third Tigers player after Dusty Hare and John Liley to score over 1500 points for the club. Another record he claimed was to be the first player to ever have scored over 1000 points in Premiership rugby. The 2001-02 season saw Tim become the first player in league history to win five successive league winners medals, however his season was marred by a horrific facial injury, from which he has fortunately fully recovered. The 2000-01 season saw Tim in terrific form amassing 486 individual points to break Joel Stransky's club record, having already surpassed John Liley's record of most points scored in a league season, having finished with 321 Premiership points in 1999-2000. He is now the Tigers specialist kicking coach and also the club's PRA representative.

D.o.B: **10.9.73**
P.o.B: **Liverpool**
Height: **6' 3"**
Weight: **15st 12lb**

Player Profiles

Tom Tierney Position: **Scrum Half**

D.o.B: 1.9.76
P.o.B: Limerick, Ireland
Height: 6' 0"
Weight: 14st 7lb

Tigers Debut: **24.08.02 at Bayonne v Biarritz**
Tigers Record: **11+8 apps, 5 pts**
Previous Clubs: **Garryowen, Munster**
Rep Hons: **Ireland (8)**

As a boy Tom excelled at Hurling, and only took up rugby aged 14. He played for the Garryowen club in Limerick, before being offered a contract with the province of Munster as a 20-year-old. Tom played eight matches for Munster in the Heineken Cup in seasons 1998-99 and 1999-2000, but an injury prevented him from playing for Munster against Tigers in the Heineken Cup final in 2001-02. His move to Leicester however saw him face his old team when he was named as scrum half for the quarter-final match against Munster which ended Tigers' involvement in the 2002-03 European competition. He has represented his county and skippered Ireland A, whilst his eight senior caps were all won successively at number 9 for Ireland between 1999-2000 including the whole of the 1999 Rugby World Cup until sidelined with a shoulder injury.

Fereti (Freddie) Tuilagi Position: **Wing / Centre**

D.o.B: 9.6.71
P.o.B: Apia, Samoa
Height: 5' 11"
Weight: 15st 11lb

Tigers Debut: **28.10.00 v Pontypridd**
Tigers Record: **61 apps, 70 pts**
Previous Clubs: **Marist St Joseph's (Samoa),**
Halifax Blue Sox RL, St Helens RL
Rep Hons: **Samoa (14)**

Freddie gained his first international experience on the 1991 tour to New Zealand. He was consequently selected for Samoa's '91 World Cup squad but did not feature in any of the matches. From '92 to '95 he toured with Samoa to Australia and South Africa, and was included in their '95 World Cup squad. Later that year Freddie turned professional for the Halifax Rugby League team, making 57 Super League appearances for them in two years, scoring an impressive 26 tries. In 1999 he joined St Helens RL before signing with Tigers in June 2000. He quickly became a firm favourite at Welford Road with his hard-hitting tackles and famous dreadlock hairstyle. He was recalled to the Samoan national side, touring with them in the summer of 2002 when he became one of three brothers to play for Samoa in the same test. He was selected to tour New Zealand with Samoa in the summer of 2003.

Player Profiles

Sam Vesty Position: **Fly Half**

Tigers Debut: **24.8.02 v Biarritz**

Tigers Record: **16+7 apps, 26 pts**

Rep Hons: **England U21**

A former pupil of John Cleveland College, Sam started playing rugby at age 10 having been inspired by his father (who played at prop for the Tigers). His talent resulted in appearances for Leicestershire at U14, U16 & U18 level as well as for Midlands U18 and England U18. Sam graduated through the Tigers' U21 team and Tigers Extras before joining the first team squad at their training camp in France in August 2001. He accompanied the team to France again the next summer, earning a first team debut as a second half replacement in the Orange Cup game against Biarritz, making him the fourth generation of his family to play for Tigers. Sam was one of three Tigers youngsters in the England squad that competed in the IRB U21 World Championship in South Africa in the summer of 2002. Sam was propelled into the first team for the 2002-03 season, acquitting himself well in the pivotal role of fly half and gaining his Player's 20 games tie, as well as picking up both the Supporters' and Players' awards for Young Player of the Season. Sam has played for the Leicestershire 2nd team and Leicestershire U19 at cricket.

D.o.B: **26.11.81**

P.o.B: **Leicester**

Height: **6' 0"**

Weight: **13st 10lb**

Julian White Position: **Prop**

Previous Clubs: **Hawke's Bay (NZ), Crusaders (NZ), Bridgend, Saracens, Bristol Shoguns**

Rep Hons: **England (14)**

Prop Julian White has gained all his England caps on the tighthead side of scrum since his debut in Pretoria on 17 June 2000. England lost that game but have only lost one other (vs Ireland in Dublin October 2001) when White has been in the team. As well as the trip to South Africa he toured with England to North America in 2001, playing in all three tests against Canada and the USA. Julian has made five appearances for England A, and is one of a select band of only three England capped players who have appeared in the Southern Hemisphere's Super-12 tournament. He made his sole Super-12 appearance as a replacement for Crusaders against Natal in April 1997 whilst in New Zealand playing for Hawke's Bay, for whom he made his debut in August 1996. Along with Martin Johnson he is one of only two current England test players to have appeared in the NZ Provincial Championship. Returning to the UK, White played for Bridgend in 1998-99 before switching to Saracens. He joined Bristol Shoguns at the start of the 2002-03 season playing for them in both the Zurich Premiership and Heineken Cup competitions.

D.o.B: **14.5.73**

P.o.B: **Plymouth**

Height: **6' 1"**

Weight: **18st**

BIGGER BETTER

W 3

U21 Season Review

The 2002-03 season was the most successful in the history of Tigers U21s. Not only did they lead the Zurich U21 league from the outset, but they also provided England with six players and the Tigers first team with eight players.

The season culminated with a 43-10 win over closest rivals Gloucester at Welford Road. In front of a record crowd the team put on a sparkling display of rugby to clinch the league title, ten points clear of second placed Gloucester.

The U21 season got off to a great start with 15 consecutive league wins, finally coming unstuck away to a strong Gloucester side in February. Over the course of the season the team notched up an impressive 20 wins in 22 league matches. Highlights included the 52-7 victory at home to Saracens, a 55-17 away win over London Wasps and a 54-8 home win over London Irish.

Aside from the Zurich U21 league, the team was involved in several friendly matches. They played against Rotherham, Leeds Tykes and also in a Boxing Day charity match against Northampton Saints. The side, officially titled "Tigers Emerging" played at Franklins Gardens in front of a paying crowd of over 5,000. Dan Hipkiss scored two tries, with Luke Myring

adding a penalty and conversion to secure a 15-12 victory. The match raised funds for local charities in both Northampton and Leicester.

Several U21 players got a taste of senior squad rugby early on in the season; Dan Hipkiss, John Holtby, Adam Billig, James Buckland and Sam Vesty were all involved in pre-season matches in France. Of course, Sam went on to become a regular first team squad member. During the season Luke Abraham, Peter Cook, Ben Gerry and Will Skinner also made their first team debuts. Will started in the Leeds game in April and became the 16th academy player to represent the first team since its inception!

Former Leicester and England captain, and current U21 backs coach Paul Dodge saw this "outstanding season" as the fruition of a four year programme. "Many of the players in this season's U21 side have been with us for several years and have progressed through the Youth team. We are starting to reap the rewards of many years hard work."

Paul's coaching partner is ex-Tigers team mate, veteran lock Tom Smith. As forwards coach he is responsible for the pack that dominated the U21 league all season. He feels this team has worked hard and grown together as a group of players. He adds,

"The forwards' ability to support the ball carrier, pass the ball out of the tackle and to stay on their feet has been the major improvement this season."

A further defining feature of this season has been the introduction of strength and conditioning coach Chris Tombs to the coaching team. Prior to joining us Chris was working with the England Rugby Union for Women. He has fitted in well and by improving the players' strength, stamina and agility has made a valuable contribution to the team's performance.

Academy bosses Andy Key and Dusty Hare see cause for celebration in the fact that the Tigers U21s provided the England team with six players this year. Peter Cook, James Hamilton, Dan Hipkiss, Michael Holford, John Holtby and Tim Taylor were all capped at U21 level. "This is a great achievement for the players and is just reward for the hard work they have put in over the years", says a thrilled Dusty.

The U21s are already looking forward to new challenges. The loss of international players to the World Cup means that more of the U21 stars will be given the opportunity to prove themselves on the first team stage. There is also every reason to feel optimistic about next season's U21 side. We look forward to seeing more players come through the Youth system and continue the success of this season's U21 squad!

U21s XV Results			
Aug 31	Worcester	H	29-28
Sep 7	Harlequins	A	10-20
Sep 13	Sharks	H	37-23
Sep 21	Newcastle Falcons	A	11-17
Sep 28	Bristol Shoguns	H	30-22
Oct 5	Bath	A	6-27
Oct 2	London Wasps	A	17-55
Oct 19	Leeds Tykes	A	3-15
Oct 25	Saracens	H	52-7
Nov 23	London Irish	H	54-8
Nov 30	Northampton Saints	A	10-38
Dec 7	London Wasps	H	32-8
Dec 26	Northampton Saints	A	12-15
Feb 1	Bath	H	20-16
Feb 8	Bristol Shoguns	A	18-40
Feb 22	Leeds Tykes	H	31-38
Feb 28	Gloucester	A	28-15
Mar 15	Rotherham	H	29-8
Apr 2	Sharks	A	21-19
Apr 5	Newcastle Falcons	H	23-15
Apr 19	Harlequins	H	24-18
Apr 26	Worcester	A	17-39
May 9	Gloucester	H	43-10

Key: ■ Home Fixtures ▢ Away Fixtures

U21 League 2002-03								
Team	P	W	D	L	F	A	BP	Pts
Leicester Tigers	22	20	0	2	674	291	16	96
Gloucester	22	18	1	3	584	339	12	86
Newcastle Falcons	22	15	1	6	513	357	13	75
London Wasps	22	12	1	9	584	536	16	66
Sale Jets	22	13	0	9	520	397	12	64
Bath Rugby	22	11	0	11	495	466	12	56
NEC Harlequins	22	10	0	12	505	576	11	51
Bristol Shoguns	22	8	2	12	534	408	13	49
Worcester	22	8	0	14	463	593	12	44
London Irish	22	6	3	13	407	517	9	39
Northampton Saints	22	6	0	16	390	604	7	31
Saracens	22	1	0	21	145	730	2	6

Zurich U21 Championship 2002-03
Wednesday 9th April 2003
Leicester Tigers 43-10 Gloucester

Tigers Youth

If you reviewed the season's results it would at first appear that the U19 team had mixed fortunes, yet there is much more to it than meets the eye.

What makes an U19 match really interesting is the fact that often players will play out of position, for example a wing might play at centre to give a greater understanding of their role on the pitch. The learning process is continually emphasised and whilst performance is central, winning isn't everything. The valuable experience that has been gained stands all the youth squad in great stead for next season.

The game of the season for the youth side was against England U18s at Welford Road and produced a hard fought match from which the Tigers emerged victorious.

England Representatives
England U19
Matt Hampson, Nathan Jones, Tom Ryder, Will Skinner
England Sevens
Will Skinner
England U18 Schools (1st September)
Matt Cornwell, Tom Gregory, Joe Wheeler
England U18 Schools (1st January)
Tom Croft
U18 Clubs
Craig Faulks

Date: Sunday 16th March 2003	
Tigers Youth	**17**
England Schools U18	**6**

The first half started very strongly for the Schools and they were rewarded with a penalty to take a 0-3 lead. Tigers hit back but missed several chances to score until Steve Bewick charged down a kick, then retrieved the ball to score under the posts, converted by Malcolm Reilly. During the first half the schools had most of the possession, but the Leicester defence was solid so held onto a 7-3 lead at half time.

The second half started with the Schools on top again, and they dropped a goal to close the gap to 7-6. However, as the game went on the Tigers started to take control, an excellent drive by the forwards from a lineout led to an unconverted try scored through Steve Bewick. The Tigers backs started to make more breaks, one excellent break by Alex Dodge led to the last try to be scored by Oliver Winter to finish the match 17-6 to the Tigers.

U19 League 2002-03

Team	P	W	D	L	F	A	BP	Pts
Worcester	10	8	0	2	224	119	5	37
Leicester Tigers	14	7	0	7	257	220	9	37
London Irish	9	7	0	2	171	111	3	31
London Wasps	13	6	0	7	227	211	5	29
NEC Harlequins	13	7	0	6	242	225	4	32
Bath Rugby	12	6	0	6	185	197	4	28
Leeds Tykes	14	5	0	9	242	266	8	28
Bristol Shoguns	8	5	0	3	135	100	2	22
Gloucester RFC	4	2	0	2	67	73	0	8
Northampton Saints	6	1	0	5	96	149	2	6
Saracens	7	1	0	6	46	224	0	4

Tigers Youth

This last year has been the first full season of the Leicester Tigers England Rugby Academy. The first step in a player's development now becomes the Elite Player Development Centres (EPDC). Leicester Tigers' four EPDC's share the responsibility for a geographical district that covers Leicestershire, Nottinghamshire, Derbyshire, Lincolnshire, Staffordshire and Norfolk. Our EPDCs work with players from U14 to U16 age groups and meet fortnightly to work on core rugby skills. Players continue to train and play with their club, as well as represent their county and England, if selected.

Successful players will progress into the Leicester Tigers England Rugby Academy, and hopefully onto the Leicester Tigers and England senior sides.

After U16 level, those players with the greatest potential are invited to join the Leicester Tigers England Rugby Academy as apprentices. They become full members of the academy; exposed to the rugby development, body management and education components of the programme.

This year the development system that Tigers has installed is showing its strength - whereas seven players are normally taken annually from the development squad to the academy, this year 11 development players have undertaken the transition.

One of the highlights of the season for Rugby Development Co-ordinator Dusty Hare is the development of Tigers lock Craig Faulks. Craig demonstrates what can be achieved through hard work and commitment – representing England U18 clubs. Emerging prop Matt Hampson playing for the England U19 squad and flanker Will Skinner with six appearances under his belt for the first team, both provide good benchmarks to aspire to.

New Apprentices
Tom Youngs
Ben Pienaar
Sam Herrington
Oliver Dodge
Alex Shaw
James Fouracre
James Metcalfe

England Representatives
England U16
Ben Pienaar, James Metcalfe, Tom Youngs
England U16A
Damien Reilly, Alex Shaw

EPDC	Region Covered	Location	Head Coach
North	Nottinghamshire, Derbyshire and Lincolnshire	Newark RFC Nottinghamshire	John Liley
South	Leicestershire	Oval Park, Oadby, Leicester	Troy Thacker
East	Norfolk	Swaffham RFC, Norfolk	Jon Curry
West	Staffordshire	Staffordshire University, Stafford	Tosh Askew

The All New

Tigers
Weather
Lottery

LEICESTER
TIGERS

HOW THE LOTTERY WORKS

The lottery is really fun to play. Simply select six lucky numbers (between 0-9) to play in our daily lottery (5 days a week 52 weeks a year). Every day we will take the last digit in Fahrenheit as reported in the Daily Telegraph for six locations and scan all the entries to see who has won.

THE PRIZE STRUCTURE

Match **3** Numbers and **YOU WIN £2**
Match **4** numbers and **YOU WIN £20**
Match **5** numbers and **YOU WIN £200**
Match **6** numbers and **YOU WIN £10,000**

HOW MUCH WILL IT COST?

Each six number entry costs £4 every four weeks (equal to just 20p per day).

HOW DO I KNOW IF I HAVE WON?

Winning numbers will be published daily on www.leicestertigers.com and in the local media.
You don't even need to check, prizes are automatically posted to you.

ARE THE PRIZES GUARANTEED?

Yes, all prizes are guaranteed. The system is insured by Lloyds of London.

HOW DO I ENTER?

Simply contact Paul Hayes at Leicester Tigers on 0116 2171 226 and join today.

SUPPORT US
AND WIN UP TO
£10,000 DAILY

Join online at www.leicestertigers.com

Head of Rugby Development: Andy Key
for biography see page 107

Dusty Hare
Position: **Rugby Development Co-ordinator**

Dusty was a professional cricketer from 1971-76 before seeing the ligh
and moving to rugby union. He joined Tigers in 1976 as fullback and wa
the world's highest point scorer, achieving 7,137 points in total, wit
4,507 for Tigers alone. He was also capped 25 times for England and wa
a British Lion.

He served on the Barbarian Committee between 1989-92 and wa
awarded an MBE in 1989. In 1993 Dusty took on the role of Director c
Rugby at Nottingham before coming back to Tigers in 1994 a
Development Co-ordinator.

Before becoming a full time coach, Dusty was a farmer. He also ha
an honorary Bachelor of Arts degree from Leicester Univerisity (1990).

Paul Dodge
Position: **Backs Coach**

Paul joined Tigers' Youth Team in 1973 and moved to the first tear
squad in 1975. His playing career at Tigers saw him appear in 43
matches as well as being capped for England in 1978.

He featured in two British Lions Tests in 1980 in South Africa an
was captain for England in 1985 as well as Tigers captain in the 87/8
season when they won the Courage League. From 1993 to 1996 Pau
coached the Tigers backs before moving to the academy as U21s back
coach in 1998.

He now works as academy coach and owns the family business c
restoration bookbinding.

Academy Coaches

Mike Penistone
Position: **Specialist Defence Coach**
D.o.B: **27.12.1950**

After playing for Moderns RFC (Nottingham) and Nottinghamshire County, Mike coached England Students rugby league, Great Britain Students rugby league as well as Nottingham RUFC, Cambridge University RL and Trent Polytechnic RL. He holds an Australian rugby league level 3 coaching badge.

His coaching influences are Peter Corcoran, ARL Director of Coaching, Chalkie White and Bill Gardner of the Brisbane Broncos. He has a Bachelor of Education degree.

Stuart Redfern
Position: **Forwards Coach**
D.o.B: **16.06.1961**

Stuart has played in 324 first team matches since joining Tigers in 1976. He has also played in ten Midlands Division games and been capped at England U23 level as well as receiving a senior cap in 1984.

He now coaches both academy teams and has the RFU level 3 coaching award. He used to work as a mechanical engineer.

Academy Coach: Glenn Gelderbloom
for biography see page 118

Academy Coaches

Tom Smith
Position: **Forwards Coach**
D.o.B: **27.12.1964**

Tom joined Tigers in 1980 and notched up 184 games for the first team. He has also coached the Extras for two years and is currently in his fifth season coaching the academy teams.

For six and a half years he was a rugby development officer in Leicestershire and he is also a PE teacher at Lancaster School. He has the RFU Intermediate coach, RFU coaching award and is currently undertaking the RFU level four programme.

Chris Tombs
Position: **Strength and Conditioning Coach**
D.o.B: **21.10.1971**

Before joining Tigers, Chris worked with the England Women's Rugby Union squad for two years, preparing them for the 2002 World Cup. He has also done various conditioning programmes for county cricketers, boxers and rugby players.

He has a degree in Human Movement Studies, an MSc in Sport & Exercise Science and is also a British Olympic Associate strength & conditioning specialist.

Ruth Cross
Position: **Physiotherapist**
D.o.B: **23.04.1968**

Ruth has a BSc (Hons) in Sport Administration & Science and a Graduate Diploma in Physiology. She is a state registered physiotherapist.

From 1993-2001 Ruth worked for Leicester Royal Infirmary and in 1994-95 was physiotherapist for South Leicester RFC before joining the Tigers in 1995. She now runs her own clinic in Oadby.

Academy Profiles

Joseph Ajuwa
Pos: Winger
D.o.B: 25.1.83
P.o.B: Layos, Algeria
Height: 6' 2"
Weight: 15st 5lb
Joined: Nov 2002
Education: Coventry University

Yomi Akinyemi
Pos: Winger
D.o.B: 5.10.83
P.o.B: London
Height: 6' 1"
Weight: 14st 4lb
Joined: July 2002
Education:
Loughborough University
Rep Hons: England U16 A

Tom Armstrong
Pos: Winger/Centre
D.o.B: 10.1.85
P.o.B: Melton Mowbray
Height: 5' 8"
Weight: 13st 2lb
Joined: 2001/2002
Education:
Loughborough College

James Bardgett
Pos: Back
D.o.B: 10.1.85
P.o.B: Keighley
Height: 5' 8"
Weight: 12st 3lb
Joined: 2002
Occupation: Joiner

Mark Bartlett
Pos: Prop
D.o.B: 3.3.85
P.o.B: Leicester
Height: 6' 1"
Weight: 18st 9lb
Joined: 2001/2002
Education:
Queen Elizabeth College

Steven Bewick
Pos: Back Row
D.o.B: 5.12.83
P.o.B: Leamington Spa
Height: 6' 0"
Weight: 13st 12lb
Joined: Aug 2002
Education:
Nottingham University

Academy Profiles

Ian Brewer
Pos: Back Row
D.o.B: 27.9.83
P.o.B: Taunton
Height: 6' 4"
Weight: 15st 6lb
Joined: 2002
Education:
Nottingham University
Rep Hons:
South West U18 Schools

Ben Chamberlin
Pos: Back Row
D.o.B: 17.7.83
P.o.B: Louth
Height: 6' 0"
Weight: 14st 7lb
Joined: 1999/2000
Education:
Brooksby Melton College

Peter Clarke
Pos: Back Row
D.o.B: 29.11.82
P.o.B: Newport
Height: 6' 0"
Weight: 14st 10lb
Joined: 2001/2002
Education:
Loughborough University
Rep Hons: Welsh Exiles U21,
Wales U21 A

Rob Cooke
Pos: Lock
D.o.B: 5.8.83
P.o.B: Dewsbury
Height: 6' 5"
Weight: 16st 4lb
Joined: 2001/2002
Education: Full time training
Rep Hons:
England U18 Schools

Daniel Cooper
Pos: Centre
D.o.B: 17.4.85
P.o.B: London
Height: 6' 0"
Weight: 13st
Joined: Sep 2002
Education: Arundel School
Rep Hons: Hong Kong Schools

Matt Cornwell
Pos: Full Back
D.o.B: 16.1.85
P.o.B: Leicester
Height: 6' 1"
Weight: 14st
Joined: Sep 2000
Education: Oakham
Rep Hons:
England U18 Schools

Academy Profiles

Thomas Croft
Pos: Lock
D.o.B: 7.11.85
P.o.B: Basingstoke
Height: 6' 5"
Weight: 14st
Joined: Sep 2002
Education: Oakham
Rep Hons:
South East Schools U16

Alex Dodge
Pos: Centre
D.o.B: 17.11.84
P.o.B: Leicester
Height: 6' 2"
Weight: 15st
Joined: 2000
Education:
Queen Elizabeth College

Rob Dumbleton
Pos: Lock
D.o.B: 3.11.83
P.o.B: Watford
Height: 6' 7"
Weight: 17st 7lb
Joined: 2002
Education:
Nottingham University
Rep Hons:
South East Schools U18

Craig Faulks
Pos: Lock
D.o.B: 21.10.85
P.o.B: Burton-Upon-Trent
Height: 6' 6"
Weight: 17st 10lb
Joined: 2002
Education:
Loughborough College

Richard Forbes
Pos: Winger
D.o.B: 11.8.84
Education:
Leicester Grammar

Chris Fores
Pos: Lock
D.o.B: 3.7.84
Height: 6' 5"
Weight: 15st 13lb
Joined: July 2002
Occupation:
Parts Sales Person

Academy Profiles

Stuart Friswell
Pos: Hooker
D.o.B: 12.1.83
P.o.B: Rugby
Height: 5' 10"
Weight: 15st 6lb
Joined: 1999/2000
Occupation:
YMCA Personal Trainer
Rep Hons: England U19

Steven Glitherow
Pos: Centre
D.o.B: 8.11.82
P.o.B: Stamford
Height: 6' 0"
Weight: 14st
Joined: 1998
Education:
Loughborough University

Richard Green
Pos: Winger
D.o.B: 13.11.85
P.o.B: Loughborough
Height: 5' 8"
Weight: 14st
Joined: Sept 2001
Education: Queen Elizabeth
Rep Hons:
Leicestershire Schools U18

Rob Green
Pos: Prop
D.o.B: 3.1.85
P.o.B: Leicester
Height: 5' 10"
Weight: 16st
Joined: 2001/02
Education: Oakham
Rep Hons: Midlands U16, U18

Tom Gregory
Pos: Centre
D.o.B: 13.1.85
Joined: 2001/02
Education: Oakham
Rep Hons:
England U18 Schools

Matt Hampson
Pos: Prop
D.o.B: 29.11.84
P.o.B: Leicester
Height: 6' 0"
Weight: 16st 2lb
Joined: 2000
Education:
Loughborough College
Rep Hons: England U18 Schools,
Eng U19

Academy Profiles

Joe Hill
Pos: Fly Half
P.o.B: Leicester
Height: 5' 9"
Weight: 12st 3lb
Joined: July 2002
Education: English Martyrs

David Jackson
Pos: Scrum Half
D.o.B: 6.3.83
Height: 5' 10"
Weight: 13st
Joined: 2000/01
Education:
Loughborough University

Joe Jackson
Pos: Centre
D.o.B: 4.7.86
P.o.B: Leicester
Height: 5' 10"
Weight: 13st
Joined: Sep 2000
Education: Oakham

Nathan Jones
Pos: Scrum Half
D.o.B: 24.2.84
P.o.B: Lichfield
Height: 5' 8"
Weight: 12st 6lb
Joined: 2001/02
Occupation:
YMCA Personal Trainer
Rep Hons: England U19

Nathan Jones (2)
Pos: Winger
D.o.B: 13.10.82
P.o.B: St.Asaph, N Wales
Height: 6' 2"
Weight: 14st 4lb
Joined: 2002
Education:
Loughborough University
Rep Hons:
Wales U16, U17, U18

James Lloyd-Taberer
Pos: Hooker
D.o.B: 21.12.85
P.o.B: Ontario, Canada
Height: 5' 7"
Weight: 13st
Joined: 2002/03
Education: Caludon Castle

Academy Profiles

Alex Loney
Pos: Hooker
D.o.B: 29.9.83
P.o.B: Manchester
Height: 6' 0"
Weight: 16st 7lb
Joined: 2002
Education:
De Montfort University
Rep Hons: England U18 Schools

Rory MacLean
Pos: Hooker
D.o.B: 6.8.84
P.o.B: Rugby
Height: 6' 0"
Weight: 13st 7lb
Joined: Sep 2001
Education: Rugby School
Rep Hons:
Midlands U18 Schools

David Maguire
Pos: Back Row
D.o.B: 10.10.84
P.o.B: Nuneaton
Height: 6' 0"
Weight: 15st 12lb
Joined: 2000
Education:
Loughborough College

Ronnie McLean
Pos: Centre
D.o.B: 5.6.85
P.o.B: Burbank, California, USA
Height: 6' 0"
Weight: 13st
Joined: Feb 2002
Education: Coventry West
Sixth Form College
Rep Hons: England U18 Clubs

Luke Myring
Pos: Fly Half
D.o.B: 20.12.83
P.o.B: Leicester
Height: 5' 11"
Weight: 13st 10lb
Joined: 1999
Education:
Loughborough University
Rep Hons: England U21,
N Midlands U18

Jon Neville
Pos: Prop
D.o.B: 8.4.86
Height: 6' 2"
Joined: 2000/2001
Education:
Loughborough College
Rep Hons:
County U15, U16, U18,
Midlands U16, U18

Academy Profiles

Alex Pochin
Pos: Prop
D.o.B: 25.6.85
P.o.B: Leicester
Height: 5' 11"
Weight: 15st 13lb
Joined: 2003
Education:
Loughborough University

Sam Raven
Pos: Back Row
D.o.B: 21.12.82
P.o.B: Hinckley
Height: 6' 0"
Weight: 10st 2lb
Joined: 1999/2000
Occupation:
YMCA Personal Trainer
Rep Hons:
Midlands U18 Schools

Alex Ray
Pos: Back Row
D.o.B: 14.9.83
P.o.B: Leamington Spa
Height: 6' 4"
Weight: 17st
Joined: July 2002
Education:
Loughborough University

Chris Read
Pos: Back Row
D.o.B: 19.5.84
P.o.B: Canterbury
Height: 6' 3"
Weight: 15st
Joined: 2002
Education:
Warwick University
Rep Hons:
England U18 Schools

Malcolm Reilly
Pos: Fly Half
D.o.B: 6.1.84
P.o.B: Milton Keynes
Height: 5' 10"
Weight: 12st 3lb
Joined: Sep 2002
Education:
Nottingham University

Tom Ryder
Pos: Lock
D.o.B: 23.2.85
Joined: 2001/02
Education: Uppingham
Rep Hons: England U19,
England U18 Schools

Academy Profiles

Matt Schaaf
Pos: Centre
D.o.B: 3.11.84
P.o.B: Bristol
Height: 5' 8"
Weight: 13st
Joined: Sep 2002
Education: Leicester Grammar
Rep Hons:
England U18 Schools trialist

Robert Shea
Pos: Prop
D.o.B: 30.9.83
P.o.B: Oldham
Height: 6' 1"
Weight: 18st 9lb
Education:
De Montfort Unversity
Rep Hons: NLD U18, Midlands
U16, NLD U16

Matt Smith
Pos: Fly Half
D.o.B: 15.11.85
Joined: 2002/03
Education: Oakham

Tim Taylor
Pos: Full Back
D.o.B: 4.10.82
P.o.B: Derby
Height: 5' 10"
Weight: 14st 2lb
Joined: 1999/2000
Education:
De Montfort University
Rep Hons: England U21

Ben Toft
Pos: Full Back
D.o.B: 18.3.86
P.o.B: Leicester
Height: 5' 8"
Weight: 11st 4lb
Education:
Queen Elizabeth College
Rep Hons:
County U18, Mids U18,
Eng Nth U16, Eng U16

Richard Webster
Pos: Prop
D.o.B: 1.5.84
Weight: 18st
Education:
Loughborough University

Academy Profiles

Ryan Wells
Pos: Back Row
D.o.B: 11.1.85
P.o.B: Nuneaton
Height: 6' 1"
Weight: 13st 7lb
Joined: 2002
Education:
King Edward VI College

Joe Wheeler
Pos: Back Row
D.o.B: 12.10.84
Joined: 2001/02
Education: Oakham
Rep Hons:
England U18 Schools

Chris Whitehead
Pos: Hooker
D.o.B: 9.5.86
P.o.B: Derby
Height: 5' 10"
Weight: 13st 7lb
Joined: 2002/2003
Education: Trent College
Rep Hons: England U16,
U18 Schools trialist

Ollie Winter
Pos: Full Back
D.o.B: 1.9.84 .
P.o.B: Burton-Upon-Trent
Height: 5' 10"
Weight: 12st 6lb
Joined: 2001/2002
Education: Stafford College
Rep Hons: England U18 Clubs

Aiden Woodhouse
Pos: Hooker
D.o.B: 15.7.85
P.o.B: Nuneaton
Height: 5' 9"
Weight: 13st
Joined: 2000/2001
Education:
Loughborough College
Rep Hons: County U14, U16,
U18, Midlands U16, U18

Alex Wright
Pos: Scrum half
D.o.B: 23.6.86
P.o.B: Leicester
Height: 5' 8"
Weight: 11st 5lb
Joined: 2000/2001
Education:
Queen Elizabeth College
Rep Hons: County U14, U16,
U18, Midlands U16, U18

Academy Profiles

Christopher Wyles
Pos: Centre
D.o.B: 13.9.83
P.o.B: USA
Height: 6' 0"
Weight: 14st
Joined: Sep 2002
Education:
Nottingham University
Rep Hons:
Middlesex U18 schools

New Academy Players

Billy Blair

Dan Cole

Oliver Dodge

James Fouracre

Sam Herrington

Marc Howgate

Craig Hughes

James Metcalfe

Michael Pearson

Harry Pick

Ben Pienaar

Alex Shaw

Tom Youngs

Stadium Bar Guide

Bars & Restaurants

1. Barbarians Lounge

2. Tiger Bar

3. European Suite

4. Leicestershire Room

5. Captain's Bar

6. Droglites

7. Dusty's Bar

8. Underwood Suite

9. Lions Bar

10. Deano's Bar

11. ABC Bar

12. Crumbie Lounge

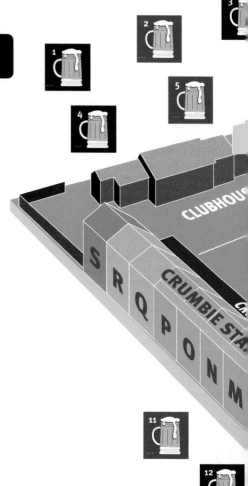

Corporate Areas

Public Areas

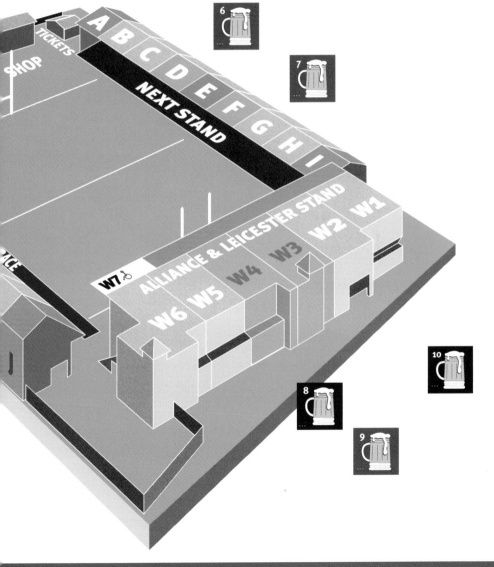

Tickets

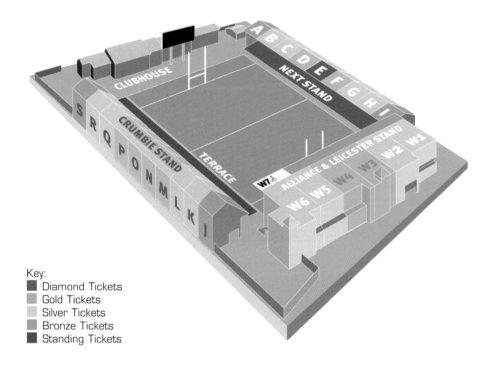

Key:
- ■ Diamond Tickets
- ▨ Gold Tickets
- □ Silver Tickets
- ▩ Bronze Tickets
- ■ Standing Tickets

Price Band	Adult	Concessions	Juniors	Family*
Diamond	£28	£25	£20	-
Gold	£25	£21	£17	-
Silver	£21	£17	£14	£56
Bronze	£19	£15	£9	£47
Standing	£15	£13	£6	£36

Key: * A Family ticket consists of two adults and two children

Tickets

The Leicester Tigers ticket office is not just for the sale of home tickets, they also stock a limited selection of away tickets for each match, and if you are a season ticket holder or a member you are entitled to apply for tickets for the England home internationals on a ballot basis.

Don't forget the legendary Barbarians fixture has returned to the Tigers rugby calendar. The United Nations of Rugby will be visiting Leicester again this season - the provisional date for this popular fixture is March 5, at 7.45pm, call now to reserve your seats as this match is not included in the season ticket.

Like last season we are expecting many of the games to sell out, so if you require tickets for yourself or your friends - book now to avoid disappointment!

For all the latest tickets and travel information check www.leicestertigers.com

Ticket Office Opening Hours
Monday - Friday 8.30am till 5pm
Saturdays 9am till 2pm
Please note that on match days these times may vary.

Community

Leicester Tigers' community programme continues to go from strength to strength and last season was a hugely successful one for this growing department. Picking up four awards, both locally and nationally, was just reward for all the community team's hard work.

During the year, the department welcomed four new members of staff including the club's own rugby development officer, special schools co-ordinator, Tigers Learning Centre co-ordinator and a Tigers community officer based in Lincolnshire.

Alliance & Leicester Tag Rugby Programme
This three-year programme came to its conclusion last season. Having visited over 300 schools, more than 17,000 children received over 1,000 hours of tag rugby coaching by Leicester Tigers players and coaches.

This pioneering scheme introduced tag rugby to all primary schools in Leicestershire and Rutland. As part of the programme each school received three coaching sessions which prepared participants for a regional festival, with the winners invited to a grand final at Welford Road.

At the Sportsmatch Awards held at Twickenham, Leicester Tigers succeeded in winning the Sportsmatch Award for Best Schools Programme as well as Best Overall Programme 2002, and the great news is that Leicester Tigers and Alliance & Leicester have agreed a second three-year programme, kicking off in September 2003.

Prima Tiger Cup
The Prima Tiger Cup is open to all rugby clubs in Leicestershire in the U10s age group. Following a qualifying festival, teams were invited to Welford Road to play against one another and to experience the atmosphere in front of nearly 17,000 people. Last season's competition was a real success with Hinckley taking the title in an exciting final.

Tigers Learning Centre
Leicester Tigers Learning Centre, aimed at students from years six and eight, was opened in January 2003. The 10-week programme focuses upon literacy, numeracy and ICT using a rugby theme. The programme was expanded after Easter and now 120 children visit the centre each week.

NOF Programme

Last season the NOF programme visited 12 schools with excellent feedback. The six-week course incorporated five different themes including 'Demonstrating a skill' and 'Giving Instructions' and was designed to help improve children's interpersonal skills and raise their self-esteem and confidence. The scheme targeted children who might have had behavioural problems and were struggling at school due to various reasons.

Tigers Rugby Courses

Last season's rugby courses saw Tigers coaches travelling as far afield as Wakefield, Birmingham, Nottingham and Norfolk.

The week-long full contact rugby courses gave players aged 8-16 years the chance to experience top-quality rugby coaching in a professional environment in association with Flogas.

Players were put through their paces and could expect to play up to five hours of rugby each day. Tigers coaches developed individual skills and set pieces as participants worked towards the Tigers Five Star Award, learned about the latest training techniques and had a go at SAQ (speed, agility and quickness) training. Certificates were presented on the final afternoon in an awards ceremony.

The courses ran throughout the summer and also during the Easter and half term holidays.

To find out more about any of the Tigers rugby courses contact Leah-Anne Hall on 0116 2171 221 or email l.hall@tigers.co.uk

New for 2003/04

Tigers are extending their community programme in 2003/04 to include a pre-match coaching clinic which involves a morning of coaching with Leicester Tigers, a match ticket to the Premiership fixture that afternoon and much more.

The clinic will take place at Tigers' Oval Park training ground on the morning and will provide young players between ages of eight and 16 the opportunity to improve their rugby playing skills with Tigers coaches. The package also includes a tour of the Tigers academy facilities and a question and answer forum with a member of the Tigers first team squad.

For more information, contact Scott Clarke on 0116 2171 283 or email scott.clarke@tigers.co.uk

Members

Members' events in 2003/04 are set to be bigger and better than ever with the fun starting on September 10, when Dean Richards and John Wells will present a season preview.

Tigers will be showing all of England's games for the season as well as previewing the World Cup and Six Nations with members of the Tigers squad.

If you are not already a Leicester Tigers member you can join by contacting Paul Hayes on 0116 2171 226 or email paul.hayes@tigers.co.uk

The provisional schedule is as follows:

Live in the Tiger Bar

October 12

England's World Cup campaign kicks off v Georgia

October 18

Group match showdown England v South Africa

November 2

England v Uruguay All of England's World Cup matches will be shown live in the Tiger Bar (subject to kick off time)

Members' Events:

September 10

Season preview with Dean Richards and/or John Wells (£15)

October 8

World Cup preview (£15)

October 29

'Meet the new guys' members' evening

December 8

'World Cup warriors' - some of Tigers' World Cup players will answer your questions about the tournament (£15)

January 7

'The season so far' - hopefully captain Martin Johnson will give his assessment of the domestic season so far and look ahead to the rest of the year (£15)

February 3

'Countdown to the Six Nations' - the forthcoming Six Nations tournament will be previewed (£15)

February 25

Free members' evening (TBA)

March 24

Members' evening (TBA) (£15)

April 28

Members' Player of the Season Awards (Price and format TBA)

All members' events priced at £15 include a hot fork buffet.

Be part of our success and join Leicester Tigers members club. Our members club offers you exclusive discounts and benefits throughout the year. Tigers membership is ideal for supporters' who are unable to commit to a season ticket but want to stay in touch with the club and receive discounts on match tickets.

Without the support of our members we would not enjoy the same level of success and we would not be able to realise the unique ambitions and challenges we have set ourselves.

As an official Leicester Tigers member you will receive:

- £1 off home match tickets
- Free quarterly newsletter
- Priority booking for home cup games
- Priority application for England home internationals
- Exclusive members only events
- Exclusive members discount in the club shop on match days
- Free tickets for Extras games played at Welford Road
- Invitation to monthly members' evenings with guest speakers
- Invitation to members' Player of the Season awards
- Discount on function room hire at Welford Road
- Discount on Christmas party bookings at Welford Road
- Exclusive members card

Membership is based on and an annual subscription and costs £25 per year. To join, contact Paul Hayes now on 0116 2171 226 or email paul.hayes@tigers.co.uk

Adams Junior Tiger Club

The Adams Junior Tiger Club is a supporters' club especially for Tigers fans up to the age of 14 years old. Our club president is Tigers star, Harry Ellis. We have loads of fun on match days and get to meet Tigers players when they come to visit us in our clubhouse.

As an Adams Junior Tiger Club member you get:
- The chance to be matchday mascot
- Free Adams Junior Tiger Club gift
- Exclusive membership card
- Entry to the Adams Junior Tiger clubhouse with computers and games
- £1 off all home matches (when booked in advance)
- Free face painting at home games
- Exclusive members events
- The chance to interview a player
- Exclusive 15% discount on Adams childrenswear upon production of your membership card (in participating stores)
- Free quarterly newsletter
- Pre-match parade at the first home game of the season with Welford and JT
- Adams Junior Tiger Club pages in the matchday programme with birthday wishes
- Birthday card

Adams Junior Tiger Club

New for 2003-04
New for next season, Leicester Tigers will be holding regular Adams Junior Tiger Club outings. Each month, Welford and JT have got something great lined up for you that includes a summer barbecue, visits to Twickenham, American Adventure, Snibston Discovery Park and much more, finishing with a Tigers sports day at the end of the season.

As soon as events are confirmed, we will contact all our members inviting them to take part, so don't miss out - join our club today.

Be A Matchday Mascot
As a member of the Adams Junior Tiger Club you get the chance to be the match day mascot and lead the Tigers team out at Welford Road. Not only that, you will also be given your own kit including shirt, shorts and socks to run out onto the pitch. This once in a lifetime chance is available exclusively to our members, who are picked at random or are one of the lucky winners of one of our newsletter competitions.

Clubhouse
As an Adams Junior Tiger Club member you gain entry to our special clubhouse before every home match. Pop in and meet your friends while you enjoy free food, drinks, fun and games. We even have special visitors from the first team squad who meet us every home game.

Free Face Painting
Get your face painted for free in the clubhouse on match days.

Birthdays
To celebrate your birthday, the Adams Junior Tiger Club will send you a special card and give you a birthday mention on our pages in the match day programme.

As a member of Adams Junior Tiger Club you can hold your birthday party at Welford Road with Welford and JT. Enjoy a great day with your mates as you play games and stuff your face full of food. We will even give you a goody bag to take home with you jam-packed with Tigers goodies.

Join Us
Joining the best junior supporters' club in the country costs just £15 for the year.
So join now by calling Paul Hayes on 0116 2171 226 or email paul.hayes@tigers.co.uk

Conference & Banqueting

Open seven days a week, Welford Road is a unique venue for business or pleasure, retaining the nostalgia and heritage of a world famous rugby club within modern facilities and luxurious surroundings.

Since opening as a conference and banqueting venue in 1998, Welford Road has fast established itself as one of the premier conference venues in the East Midlands.

Conference & Banqueting

Christmas 2003

What better way to celebrate Christmas than in the familiar surroundings of Welford Road. Whether you are planning a staff outing, a family party or a Christmas celebration with friends, there is a festive package to suit you at Welford Road.

Why not try something a bit different this year with one of our casino nights or dance the night away to the sounds of our resident house band. Remember we will tailor the party to suit your needs, but places are limited, so make your reservation now by calling Jackie, Mandy or Nina on 0116 2171 278.

Located in the heart of England, the stadium is easily accessible from the motorway network and East Midlands Airport and is within walking distance of Leicester Mainline Railway Station.

As a training venue our Alliance & Leicester Stand offers a unique facility, which can accommodate up to 150 delegates in our main conference room with up to 15 breakout rooms. There is also on site secure car parking with closed circuit TV.

Tigers' standard conference packages suit the needs of many customers, but the conference and banqueting staff are always happy to tailor any package to suit individual requirements.

And Welford Road isn't just open for business. If you are looking for somewhere to hold a birthday or family party, host a special event, or just want a room to have a disco and let your hair down, there is a function room that will suit your needs. A variety of menus ranging from a finger buffet to a full sit down dinner means that there is a price range to suit all pockets.

Whatever extras you require for your function, the conference and banqueting team are happy to work with you to arrange additions such as musical entertainment, bar extensions, floral or balloon arrangements for the tables, themed evenings and personalised table plan and menus.

The club also caters for wedding receptions, Christmas parties and private functions as well as offering a room-only rate.

log on to....

www.leicestertigers.com was re-launched in March 2003 and now boasts the largest content in the Premiership.

In Touch With Tigers
Be the first to know all the Leicester Tigers news this season with TigerTXT, the club's exclusive mobile phone messaging service.

Whether you want to find hear about Tigers' latest signings or keep up to date with the tour news and the summer training, sign up now. During the season you can sign up for home and away match updates to get half time and full time scores on the whistle.

The system is so easy to use and is flexible to suit your needs. To register for TigerTXT, or for more information, log onto www.leicestertigers.com and click on the flashing icon on the right hand side of the page.

Register Your Support
Leicester Tigers has introduced a registration system to www.leicestertigers.com for the 2003/04 season.

The system means that the club is far better equipped to communicate with its supporters and it will provide Tigers with the ability to improve standards of customer service.

There have also been some problems on the chat forum with a small minority of fans from other clubs who have misused it and caused offence to families who read its contents. Registration will allow the webmaster to deactivate those individuals' accounts which will make it extremely difficult for them to re-register.

You will only need to register once which should take you no more than two minutes and will give you access to the whole site.

By collecting this information Tigers will be able to assist supporters with specific needs, for example, a group of supporters from London who would like to organise group travel to home and away games.

As a registered user you will be in control of your account and you can update whether you wish to receive information from the club such as Tigerzine and in what format (HTML or Text), through the 'My Details' section of the website.

So don't miss out on all the latest news, views and information from Leicester Tigers. Log on now.

Tigerzine

Tigers' weekly ezine keeps you up to date with all the news at Welford Road – from player updates and match information to special offers in the Tigers shop and members' events.

Tigerzine was relaunched over the summer and is now published in a full colour, easy to read format with photographs and direct links to breaking news on www.leicestertigers.com

You can sign up for Tigerzine when you register on www.leicestertigers.com

Bath Rugby

A contender for the most beautiful backdrop in Premiership rugby, Bath's Recreation Ground is set in the centre of the city's Victorian heart.

It is a shame that the same cannot be said of the facilities – its central location within the historic city has meant that all the stands are temporary. As a consequence, pray it doesn't rain, as there is little shelter within the ground.

However, its proximity to the town centre leaves it with excellent local amenities – and the tourist attractions, including the Roman Baths and photography museum, mean that it is well worth a weekend-long visit as there is plenty to see and do.

Parking is an issue and, although visitors are unlikely to find street parking close to the ground, a park and ride service operates on match days. Tigers supporters travelling to Bath are advised to buy their tickets early as due to the popularity of the old rivals fixture it often sells out.

Useful Information

Founded:
1865

Ground:
The Recreation Ground,
Bath BA2 6PW

Capacity:
8,182 (5,740 seated)

Switchboard:
01225 325200

Website:
www.bathrugby.com

Home Colours:
Blue with black and white

Change Colours:
Black with white and blue

Players In:
B.Daniel, A.Higgins, M.Lipman, P.Richards, R.Fidler, I.Clark, I.Feaunati, M.Wood, D.Bell, D.Flatman, J.Pettemerides, C.Balshen

Players Out:
G.Cooper, S.Cox, J.El Abd, N.Rouse, N.Thomas, A.Galasso, R.Chrystie, T.Voyce, E.Seveali'i, G.Thomas, S.Emms, J.Mallett, A.Long

Roll of Honour

English Champions: 1989, 1991, 1992, 1993, 1994, 1996

English Cup Winners: 1984, 1985, 1986, 1987, 1989, 1990, 1992, 1994, 1995, 1996

European Cup Winners: 1998

Previous Meetings (Leicester Tigers score first)

Venue	Date	Score
Recreation Ground	1 Feb 2003	15 - 8
Welford Road	5 Oct 2002	22 - 20
Recreation Ground	9 Mar 2002	27 - 9
Welford Road	22 Sep 2001	48 - 9
Twickenham	13 May 2001	22 - 10
Recreation Ground	26 Dec 2000	17 - 16
Welford Road	16 Dec 2000	27 - 19
Welford Road	21 May 2000	43 - 25
Recreation Ground	26 Dec 1999	13 - 3
Recreation Ground	3 Apr 1999	16 - 24

Recreation Ground

Directions

By Car
(Lambridge Park & Ride)
Leave the M4 at Junction 18 and
follow the A46 to Bath. Follow
the signs for the town centre.
The Park & Ride is at Bath
Rugby's training ground on your
left after the first set of traffic
lights.
The Park & Ride is open for all
1st XV weekend fixtures.
To go direct to the stadium, carry
on past the training ground until
you reach the junction on

London Road with Bathwick
Street. Turn left and then right
down Sydney Place. Go straight
on at the roundabout then turn
left down North Parade. The
ground is on your right.

By Rail
Bath has direct links to London,
Bristol, Cardiff, Salisbury and
Southampton.
From Birmingham and the
Midlands, there are connecting
services at Bristol Temple Meads.
National Rail enquiries: 08457 48
49 50.

By Coach
National Express services operate
between most major towns and
cities in Britain.
For further information contact
Bath Bus Station on 01225
464446 or National Express
direct on 08705 80 80 80 or visit
www.nationalexpress.com

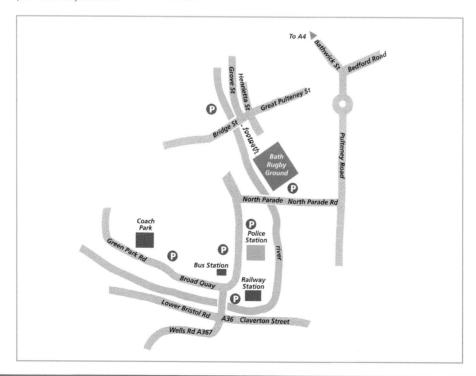

Gloucester

Useful Information

Founded:
1873
Ground:
Kingsholm, Kingsholm Road,
Gloucester GL1 3AX
Capacity:
10,800 (1,498 seated)
Switchboard:
01452 381087
Website:
www.gloucesterrugbyclub.com
Home Colours:
Cherry & White hoops
Change Colours:
Blue and Red halves
Players In:
A.Brown, P.Johnstone,
S.Brotherstone, D.McRae
Players Out:
R.Fiddler, O.Azam, L.Mercier,
C.Stuart-Smith, D.Molloy

Kingsholm, the home of Gloucester, is infamous for the raucous nature of 'The Shed'. This covered section of terracing is home to some of the most vocal supporters, nicknamed the 'The Shed'. The ground is mostly standing, so if you do require a seat, book early.

Kingsholm has excellent views of the city's cathedral, which dates back to the 12th century, and is a short walking distance from the town centre and train station.

If you're feeling more like a mouse than a man, you might like to take a peek at the home of Beatrix Potter's Tailor of Gloucester! On match days there are a number of local car parks, as well as those operated by the club.

Roll of Honour

English Championship Winners: 2002
English Cup Winners: 1972, 1978, 1982 (shared), 2003

Previous Meetings (Leicester Tigers score first)

Kingsholm	10 May 2003	13 - 31
Welford Road	15 Nov 2002	20 - 15
Welford Road	16 Mar 2002	27 - 10
Kingsholm	15 Sep 2001	40 - 18
Kingsholm	31 Mar 2001	13 - 22
Welford Road	2 Dec 2000	31 - 28
Welford Road	18 Apr 2000	24 - 13
Kingsholm	1 Oct 1999	6 - 34
Welford Road	23 Jan 1999	23 - 16
Kingsholm	19 Dec 1998	23 - 18

Kingsholm

Directions

By Car

From Midlands: From the M5 southbound, exit at junction 11 (Cheltenham south and Gloucester north). Follow A40 to Gloucester/Ross and Northern Bypass. Turn left at Longford roundabout (where A40 crosses A38) towards the City Centre. Go straight over the Tewkesbury Road roundabout and the ground is on your right after a quarter of a mile.

From South: From the M4 westbound, exit at junction 15 (Swindon) and follow the A419/417 to Gloucester. At Zoons Court roundabout follow the signs A40 to Ross and continue along Northern Bypass until you reach Longford roundabout. The as route for Midlands.

From West Country: Exit the M5 northbound at junction 11A (Gloucester) until you reach Zoons Court roundabout. Then as above.

Parking is available approx 5 minutes from the ground. Turn right at the Tewkesbury Road roundabout and follow the signs for the Park and Ride Car Park.

By Rail

Gloucester station is a 5 minute walk from the ground, and is well sign-posted.

Virgin Trains, Great Western and Central Trains all serve Gloucester from the Midlands, and there are direct services from all regions.

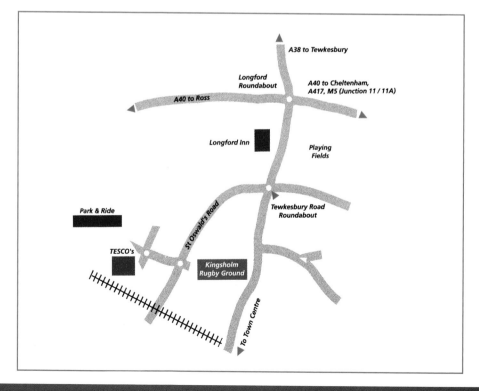

Leeds Tykes

Useful Information

Founded:

1997

Ground:

Headingley Stadium,

St Michaels Lane,

Headingley, Leeds LS6 3BR

Capacity:

23,000 (9,000 seated)

Switchboard:

0113 278 6181

Website:

www.leedsrugby.com

Home Colours:

Royal blue, black, gold & white

Change Colours:

Maroon and white

Players In:

P.Christophers, S.Morgan,
D.Rees, M.Salter, G.Powell,
C.Rigney, C.Stuart-Smith,
M.Cardey, S.Halford, D.Hodge,
S.Hooper, A.Persico, T.Walsh

Players Out:

I.Clark, I.Feaunati, C.Mather,
G.Harder, B.van Straaten,
C.Murphy

Mixing Yorkshire's three favourite sports, Headingley Stadium is host to cricket, rugby league and more recently rugby union, which means that the ground is in use all year round and in tune with the needs of its supporters.

For supporters arriving in good time for the game, the centre of Headingley offers a cornucopia of delights. Whether you go to the Original Oak, the Skyrack or one of the more trendy bars on the main street, you will be guaranteed a friendly welcome.

In less than 10 minutes you'll be back in the ground where, if you're lucky, you'll miss the pre-match entertainment which involves young girls with plastic smiles attempting to dance to the latest tunes.

Tigers supporters love terracing and you won't find a better terrace than at Headingley – in fact three sides of the ground are terraced. The South Stand offers the most accommodation, in which travelling fans are likely to outnumber the home support who prefer the seated North Stand. The South Stand is also furnished by a large bar serving draught only which means that the long queues are served surprisingly quickly.

Access to the ground is easy and parking is on the side streets – of which there are plenty – around Headingley. Regular buses serve Headingley from the city centre or you can jump on a train from Leeds to Burley which is less than 10 minutes from the ground.

Roll of Honour

National Division 1 Champions: 2000-2001

Previous Meetings (Leicester Tigers score first)		
Welford Road	26 Apr 2003	18 - 17
Headingley	31 Aug 2002	13 - 26
Welford Road	19 Apr 2002	31 - 10
Headingley	11 Nov 2001	16 - 37

Headingley

Directions

By Car

From South

Take the M62 and exit onto the M621 at junction 27. Continue along the M621 before exiting at junction 2 (signposted Headingly Stadium). Take the A643 (A58) Wetherby Road until you come to a roundabout, then follow the exit for the City Centre/Wetherby. Take the first left towards Ilkley then left again at the traffic lights into Kirkstall Road. Continue until you see Yorkshire Television on the right, and turn right at the traffic lights. Carry on straight ahead, passing another set of traffic lights, and turn left into St Michael's Lane. The stadium is on the right.

By Rail

Leeds City station is in the City Centre, and is on the Eastcoast Rail Network.

Headingly and Burley stations are approx 5 minutes away from the stadium.

By Air

Leeds and Bradford International Airport is located in the north of the city, and is served by most major European airports.

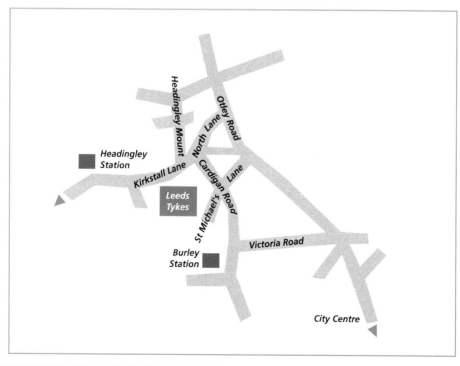

London Irish

Useful Information

Founded:
1898
Ground:
Madejski Stadium,
Reading, Berkshire RG2 0FL
Capacity:
25,000 (all seated)
Switchboard:
0118 987 9730
Website:
www.london-irish.com
Home Colours:
Green / white / green
Change Colours:
Blue / white / blue
Players In:
N.Greenstock, P.Murphy
Players Out:
M.Worsley, S.Halford

The Madejski Stadium, shared with Reading Football Club, provides London Irish with all the facilities you would expect from a ground that was used for the final of the Parker Pen Shield.

However, if you're not in the mood for Guinness or piped Irish music, the ground's isolated nature leaves you little choice. If you want to join in the craic, the post-match 'Craic in the Valley' in the North Stand occurs after all home games.

Digger the mascot is always a source of fun. If you're lucky he will be wearing his Elvis costume, along with Jumbo the Irish Wolfhound whose owners Vic and Jenny are landlords of the London Irish supporters' pub, The Swan Inn.

Although shuttle buses leave Reading station at regular intervals, visitors are advised not to leave it too late after the game, as the post match queues are horrendous. The Madejski Stadium is well served by car parking, situated close to the M4, and is unlikely to sell out.

Roll of Honour

English Cup Winners: 2002

Previous Meetings (Leicester Tigers score first)

Welford Road	3 May 2003	19 - 20
Madejski Stadium	24 Nov 2002	7 - 27
Welford Road	12 May 2002	34 - 16
Madejski Stadium	2 Dec 2001	30 - 15
Welford Road	28 Apr 2001	24 - 11
Madejski Stadium	10 Feb 2001	28 - 9
Welford Road	16 Sep 2000	33 - 20
Welford Road	25 Mar 2000	41 - 16
The Stoop	16 Oct 1999	31 - 30
Welford Road	13 Feb 1999	31 - 10

Madejski Stadium

Directions

By Car

Approaching on the M4, exit at junction 11 onto the A33 towards Reading. When you reach a roundabout, take the 2nd exit onto the Reading Relief Road, the stadium is on your left.

For parking, carry on past the stadium and turn left onto Northern Way and follow the signs for the car parks.

By Rail

Trains run from London Paddington and London Waterloo to Reading station. A shuttle bus runs from Reading station to the ground on matchdays, costing £2 for adults and £1 for children.

By Coach

National Express coaches run from London Victoria station approx every half hour. Visit www.nationalexpress.com for further information.

Mascot: Digger the Wolfhound

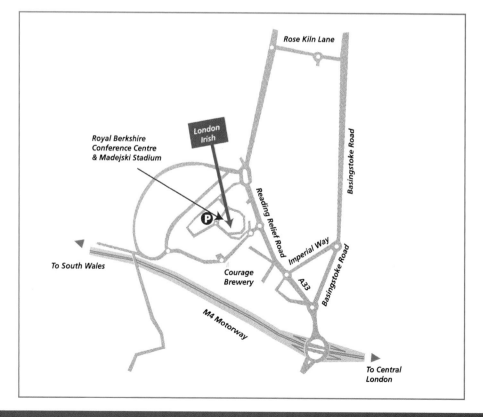

London Wasps

Useful Information

Founded:

1867

Ground:

Adams Park, Hillbottom Road,

Sands, High Wycombe,

Buckinghamshire HP12 4HJ

Capacity:

10,200 (all seated)

Switchboard:

0208 993 8298

Website:

www.wasps.co.uk

Home Colours:

Black and gold

Change Colours:

Gold and black

Players In:

T.Voyce, J.O'Connor, T.Payne

Players Out:

M.Wood, A.Kershaw

Wasps, once again, have set their wandering roots for another season at Wycombe's Adams Park. The ground is at the end of an industrial estate, surrounded on three sides by fields, and as a consequence there are no facilities within close walking distance.

Visitors can look forward to spending pre-match in the company of Sting, their feisty wasp mascot, and amazing views of the Chilterns. In the heart of Buckinghamshire, the ground is linked to the railway station by a free match day shuttle bus service which is very popular. It's worth checking their website as it contains timetables for both the shuttle and rail links.

Parking is minimal and the post match traffic tends to bottleneck. Bearing in mind that Adams Park's capacity is 10,200 it is likely that the Tigers fixture will be a sell-out again this season.

Roll of Honour

English Champions: 1990, 1997, 2003

English Cup Winners: 1999, 2000

European Shield Winners: 2003

Previous Meetings (Leicester Tigers score first)

Adams Park	27	Dec 2002	13 - 26
Welford Road	2	Nov 2002	9 - 6
Loftus Road	31	Mar 2002	24 - 36
Welford Road	8	Sep 2001	45 - 15
Welford Road	18	Nov 2000	28 - 13
Loftus Road	19	Aug 2000	24 - 22
Loftus Road	25	Jan 2000	29 - 20
Welford Road	13	Nov 1999	28 - 9
Welford Road	27	Mar 1999	16 - 6
Loftus Road	15	Nov 1998	17 - 45

Adams Park

Directions

By Car

From North

Approaching on the M1, exit onto the M25 at junction 6a (anticlockwise). Continue on the M25 until junction 16 (M40), then head to junction 4 for the A404 High Wycombe. When you reach the junction take the slip road and turn right, taking the exit for the A4010 John Hall Way. Continue on this road, which becomes New Road, until you reach a mini roundabout with a left turn on to Lane End Road. Take this left turning and continue straight ahead onto Hillbottom Road, which leads to Adams Park.

By Rail

Train services run from London Marylebone to High Wycombe.

Mascot: Sting

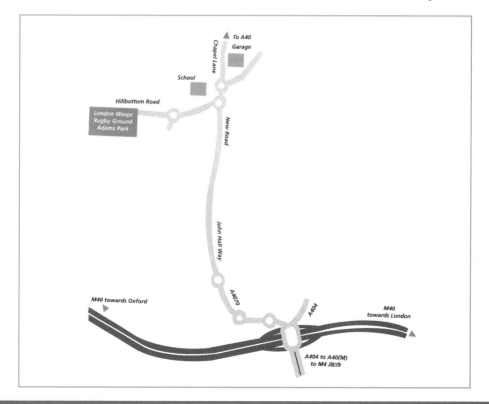

NEC Harlequins

NEC
HARLEQUINS

Useful Information

Founded:

1866

Ground:

The Stoop Memorial Ground,
Langhorn Drive,
Twickenham TW2 7SX

Capacity:

8,500 (7,450 seated)

Switchboard:

020 8410 6000

Website:

www.quins.co.uk

Home Colours:

Light blue, magenta, chocolate,
french grey, light green, & black

Change Colours:

None

Players In:

S.Taumalolo, G.Duffy, G.Harder,
A.Dunne, S.Keogh, B.Willis,
M.Worlsey

Players Out:

N.Greenstock, D.Luger, K.Wood,
A.Codling, B.Gollings, D.Griffin,
A.Mockford, D.Slemen, B.Starr,
M.Powell

The close proximity to Twickenham of Harlequins' ground – The Stoop – has meant that they have benefited from the excellent public transport access and parking facilities associated with the England ground, as well as its Rugby Museum.

Again, the temporary stands provide no shelter to the elements. However, The Stoop outshines its bigger neighbour in many ways. Deserving recommendation alone for the amount of ladies toilets – the East stand's facilities are excellent, often with a band providing post match entertainment.

The younger supporters are also well catered for with the 'Mighty Quins Village' – an adult-free zone with loads of activities and games, often frequented by Harley and Charley, the Quins' troublesome mascot bears. With this strong family focus and good travel facilities it's unsurprising that the Tigers fixture usually sells out.

Roll of Honour

English Cup Winners: 1988, 1991

European Shield Winners: 2001

Previous Meetings (Leicester Tigers score first)

Welford Road	18	May 2003	28 - 13
The Stoop	14	May 2003	23 - 26
The Stoop	19	Apr 2003	9 - 17
Welford Road	7	Sep 2002	30 - 6
The Stoop	22	Dec 2001	38 - 21
Welford Road	23	Nov 2001	23 - 18
Welford Road	14	Apr 2001	37 - 5
The Stoop	24	Nov 2000	16 - 13
The Stoop	6	May 2000	54 - 5
Welford Road	29	Dec 1999	29 - 17

The Stoop

Directions

Directions

By Car

From North

Approaching on the M1, exit onto the M25 at junction 6a (anticlockwise). Continue until you reach the junction with the M4 (junction 15), then turn off at junction 3, on to the A312 in the direction of Feltham. At the A305/A316 round-about, turn left onto the A316 Chertsey Road and follow until you see Twickenham Rugby Stadium on your left and the Stoop on the right. To reach the ground, enter through Langhorn Drive.

By Bus

Numbers 281 (from Hounslow) and 267 (from Hammersmith) run within walking distance of the stadium

By Train

Trains run from London Waterloo and Reading to Twickenham station. Follow the signposts for Twickenham Rugby Stadium upon leaving the station.

Mascot: Harley Bear

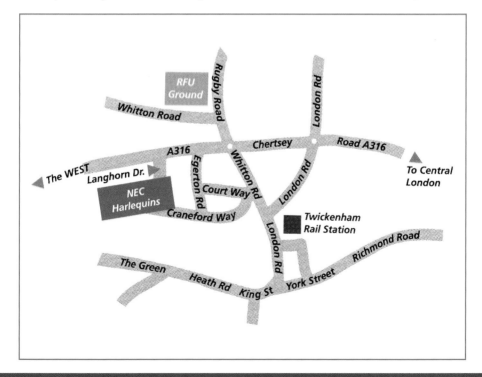

Newcastle Falcons

NEWCASTLE FALCONS

Useful Information

Founded:

1995 (Gosforth formed in 1877)

Ground:

Kingston Park, Brunton Road,
Kenton Bank Foot,
Newcastle NE13 8AF

Capacity:

10,000

Switchboard:

0191 214 5588

Website:

www.newcastle-falcons.co.uk

Home Colours:

Black with gold trim

Change Colours:

Gold with black trim

Players In:

G.Archer

Players Out:

G.Maclure, S.Brotherstone,
L.Botham

Home originally to Newcastle Gosforth, Kingston Park is on the outskirts of Newcastle. Ground improvements, including the recently developed South Stand, boost the capacity to 10,000.

Bars and amenities within the ground compensate for the lack of local facilities, although the Twin Farms pub within five minutes has a good selection of real ales and a beer garden. Pre-match entertainment includes the mascot, Flash the Falcon.

The Falcons have entered into a unique programme with Newcastle City Council, called the Green Transport Plan. The plan which is intended to cause minimum disruption to local residents as the ground is on the edge of a housing estate – means that supporters can park at Newcastle Airport and be transferred to the stadium by buses. This new initiative increases the wide range of public transport access, including the metro, which Kingston Park has to offer.

Roll of Honour

English Champions: 1998

English Cup Winners: 1976, 1977, 2001

Previous Meetings (Leicester Tigers score first)

Kingston Park	16	Mar 2003	22 - 24
Welford Road	21	Sep 2002	52 - 9
Welford Road	13	Apr 2002	20 - 12
Kingston Park	2	Sep 2001	16 - 19
Welford Road	17	Mar 2001	51 - 7
Kingston Park	27	Aug 2000	25 - 22
Welford Road	12	Feb 2000	34 - 26
Kingston Park	5	Nov 1999	12 - 12
Kingston Park	2	May 1999	21 - 12
Welford Road	12	Dec 1998	31 - 18

Kingston Park

Directions

By Car

From South

Take the M1 and turn right onto the M62 at junction 42, towards the A1. Follow the A1 all the way into Newcastle, heading for the junction for Newcastle Airport. When you reach that junction, take the Kingston Park exit then continue straight ahead over two mini roundabouts. After passing under a bridge, turn right into Brunton Road then continue until you see the ground on your left.

From West

Follow the A69 until it joins the A1, and follow signs for the Newcastle Airport junction. Then as route for South.

By Rail

GNER and Virgin Trains run services to Newcastle Central. From there, catch the Tyne and Wear Metro to Kingston Park station.

By Air

Newcastle International Airport is a short cab ride from the stadium.

Mascot: Flash the Falcon

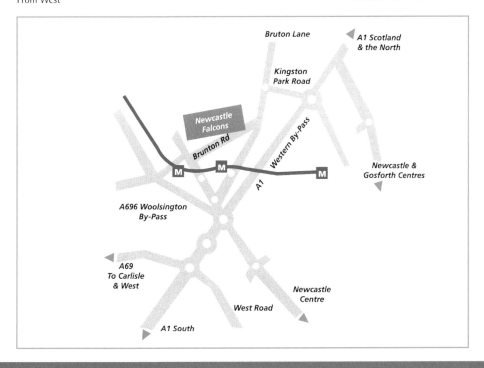

Northampton Saints

Useful Information

Founded:

1880

Ground:

Franklin's Gardens,
Weedon Road,
Northampton NN5 5BG

Capacity:

13,500 (11,500 seated)

Switchboard:

01604 751543

Website:

www.northamptonsaints.co.uk

Home Colours:

Black, green, gold hoops

Change Colours:

Gold

Players In:

M.Robinson, S.Drahm

Players Out:

M.Stewart, P.Jorgensen, I.Vass,
S.Hepher

Situated about a 10-15 minute walk from Northampton Station, Franklin's Gardens is the home of Northampton Saints Rugby Club.

Last season's Tigers fixture saw the unveiling of the new South Stand. The Tetley's Stand offers new terracing and a fine pint of draft ale. The investment by the club in the stadium has attracted England 'A' games, a Powergen Cup Semi Final and the Wildcard Final last season.

However, the facilities are not without their limitations – scoreboards are difficult to see and the toilet queues are disappointingly long at half-time and post match. The adjoining Franklin's Bar is a great meeting point prior to the game, providing a chance to sample the unique atmosphere before entering the ground.

The fixture will sell out, but is well worth the trip. If travelling by public transport, it is worth remembering that there is no direct link by train.

Roll of Honour

European Cup Winners: 2000

Previous Meetings (Leicester Tigers score first)

Welford Road	30 Nov 2002	12 - 25
Franklin's Gardens	9 Nov 2002	16 - 3
Welford Road	23 Feb 2002	17 - 6
Franklin's Gardens	13 Oct 2001	21 - 11
Welford Road	5 May 2001	17 - 13
Franklin's Gardens	10 Mar 2001	12 - 9
Welford Road	2 Sep 2000	33 - 19
Welford Road	29 Apr 2000	26 - 21
Franklin's Gardens	11 Sep 1999	24 - 46
Franklin's Gardens	13 Mar 1999	22 - 15

Franklin's Gardens

Directions

By Car

From North

Approaching on the M1, exit at junction 16 and take the A45 onto Weedon Road, which is signposted 'Town Centre'. Turn left into Ross Road and follow signs for the car park.

From South

Approaching on the M1, exit at junction 15a and follow signs for Sixfields. Turn left to join the A45 onto Weedon Road. Then as route for North.

By Rail

Silverlink trains run from Milton Keynes Central or Coventry to Northampton station. Silverlink Trains also run directly from London Euston to Northampton station.

From Northampton station, turn right and continue walking until you pass the bus station and enter a shopping area. Turn left, then left again down Abbey Street into the Northampton Saints Car Park.

Mascot: Bernie the St Bernard

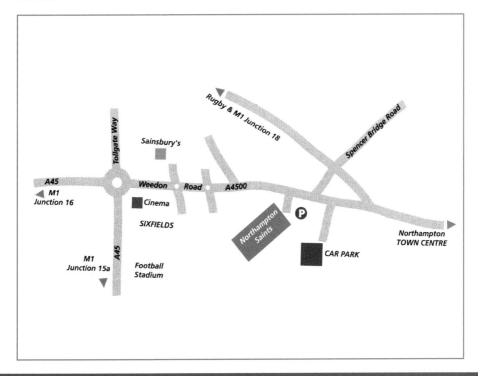

Rotherham

Useful Information

Founded:
1923
Ground:
Millmoor Ground,
Rotherham S60 1HR
Capacity:
11,499 (all seated)
Switchboard:
01709 512 434
Website:
www.rrufc.co.uk
Home Colours:
Burgundy, navy, white bands
Change Colours:
Red with navy / white shoulders
Players In:
C.Loader, C.Short, D.Jelley,
P.Smyth, G.Easterby, L.Gross,
J.Cockle, L.Starling, J.Pritchard,
J.Strange, P.Jones, G.Lewis,
A.Elliott, P.Jorgensen
Players Out:
R.Pez, A.Tooala, J.Cannon,
J.Cundick, S.Dixon, T.Foster,
M.Giacheri, A.Gravil, S.Lamont,
H.Parr, L.Wilfley

Millmoor, home to the newly promoted Rotherham – is well served by public transport, with Rotherham central train station just five minutes walk away.

It is also served well by public houses – the Tivoli and The Millmoor pubs come recommended. especially to enjoy the atmosphere and friendly banter. There is car parking specifically for away supporters close to the ground, as well as street parking.

Previous Meetings (Leicester Tigers score first)		
Clifton Lane	23 Sept 2001	20 - 6
Welford Road	6 Sept 2001	19 - 6
Welford Road	14 Nov 1997	60 - 19

Millmoor Ground

Directions

By Car

From South

Approaching on the M1, exit at junction 33. Turn right at the roundabout onto the Rotherway (signposted Rotherham A630), then left at the next roundabout onto West Bawtry Road. Continue for half a mile, then turn right at the next roundabout. Follow for approx 1 and a half miles until you reach Ickles roundabout. Go straight ahead, following the route for Doncaster A630, Barnsley. After another half a mile turn left at Masbrough roundabout to reach the stadium.

From North

Leave the M1 at junction 34 and take the second exit at the roundabout, signposted Rotherham A6109. Continue along Meadow Bank Road for approx one and a half miles, before turning right at the traffic lights into Kimberworth Road. At the T-Junction turn left to reach the stadium.

By Rail

Rotherham Central station is approx half a mile from the stadium. Arriva Trains Northern run from Sheffield or Doncaster to Rotherham Central station.

Upon leaving the station, turn left into College Road. Turn left again into Masbrough Street, then into subway. Go straight across the centre of the subway and take the stairs on the left to reach the stadium.

StationMain Street, Rotherham (0.5 Miles)

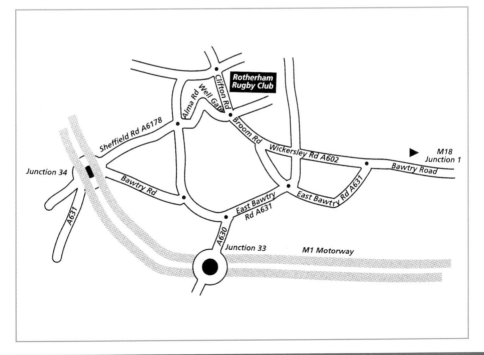

Saracens

SARACENS

Useful Information

Founded:

1876

Ground:

Vicarage Road Stadium,
Vicarage Road,
Watford, Herts WD1 8ER

Capacity:

22,000 (all seated)

Switchboard:

01923 475222

Website:

www.saracens.com

Home Colours:

Black with red shoulders

Change Colours:

Black, red and white

Players In:

E.Bergamaschi, R.Ibanez,
A.Codling, R.Kafer, S.Raiwalui,
A.Kershaw

Players Out:

C.Califano, T.Shanklin, S.Hooper,
T.Horan, A.Benazzi, M.Cairns

Vicarage Road, home of Saracens and Watford Football Club, has a capacity of 22,000 and as a consequence is unlikely to sell out.

Saracens have a unique approach to rugby entertainment – with Fez hats, a camel and a remote controlled car. When they say "it's not a game – it's an experience" they're not wrong.

The Red Lion across the road from the ground is full of Saracens and Watford memorabilia, and is a good place for a pre-match pint. Situated close to the town centre there are plenty of food and drink establishments.

If you are travelling to Saracens by car, the proximity to Watford High Street means that there are a number of city centre car parks, and two mainline train stations that serve the town.

Roll of Honour

English Cup Winners: 1998

Previous Meetings (Leicester Tigers score first)

Franklin's Gardens	31 May 2003	27 - 20
Welford Road	4 Jan 2003	23 - 18
Vicarage Road	27 Oct 2002	26 - 18
Vicarage Road	9 Feb 2002	48 - 7
Welford Road	20 Oct 2001	36 - 10
Welford Road	24 Feb 2001	56 - 15
Vicarage Road	10 Sep 2000	9 - 17
Welford Road	22 Jan 2000	48 - 20
Vicarage Road	5 Dec 1999	20 - 36
Welford Road	17 Apr 1999	25 - 18

Vicarage Road

Directions

By Car

From North

Leave the M1 at junction 5, taking the third exit from the roundabout and follow signs to Watford Town Centre. When joining the ring road get into the middle lane, before moving into the left lane after the second set of traffic lights. Follow signs for Watford General Hospital, which is next to Vicarage Road.

From West

Leave the M25 at junction 19, and follow the A411 Hempstead Road, signposted Watford. Go straight over the first roundabout, then left at the second. Follow the signs towards Watford General Hospital, which is next to Vicarage Road.

By Rail

Watford High Street station is approx 10 minutes walk from the stadium. North London Railway trains run from London Euston station.

By London Underground

Watford tube station is approx 20 minutes walk from the stadium, on the Metropolitan Line.

Mascot: Sarrie the Camel

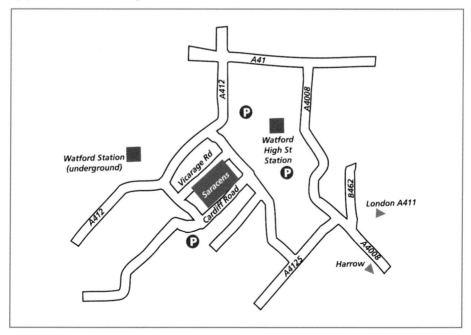

Sharks

Useful Information

Founded:

1861

Ground:

Edgeley Park, Hardcastle Road, Edgeley, Stockport SK3 9DD

Capacity:

5,678 (3,132 seated)

Switchboard:

0161 283 1861

Website:

www.salesharks.com

Home Colours:

Royal Blue shirt with navy band

Change Colours:

Black with green band

Players In:

A.Sheridan, A.Newton, J.White, B.van Straaten, M.Cairns, M.Simpson-Daniel

Players Out:

R.Wilks, A.Elliott, S.Lines, C.Marais, J.Thorp

This season sees the Sharks moving to the home of Stockport County – Edgeley Park.

A five minute walk from the town centre, the stadium is well-served by public transport. Buses 9 to 11 stop by the ground and Stockport railway station is only half a mile away.

For supporters travelling to the ground by car, parking is available in the precinct car park off Castle Street.

The ground is somewhat of an unknown entity for rugby, but the football clan recommend that supporters should steer clear of the open away terrace in poor weather as there is absolutely no protection from the elements.

Roll of Honour

European Shield Winners: 2002

Previous Meetings (Leicester Tigers score first)		
Welford Road	6 Apr 2003	33 - 20
Heywood Road	13 Sep 2002	16 - 29
Welford Road	27 Dec 2001	33 - 10
Heywood Road	17 Nov 2001	37 - 3
Welford Road	6 Mar 2001	24 - 12
Heywood Road	30 Sep 2000	17 - 17
Heywood Road	22 Apr 2000	48 - 13
Welford Road	25 Sep 1999	18 - 3
Heywood Road	24 Apr 1999	41 - 17
Welford Road	17 Oct 1998	31 - 15

Edgeley Park

Directions

By Car

From South

Leave the M6 at junction 19 (towards Manchester Airport, Stockport A55), then turn right at the roundabout onto the A556. After approx four miles you reach a roundabout, turn right onto the M56 (towards Manchester). After a approx a further seven miles, exit the M56 and join the M60 (signposted Stockport, Sheffield). Leave the M60 at junction 1 and follow the signs to Cheadle and Stockport County FC at the roundabout. Continue straight ahead at the first set of traffic lights, then right at the next set (keep following signs for Stockport County FC). After a mile, turn left onto the B5465 Edgeley Road, then after another mile turn right into Dale Street. Take the second turning on the left into Hardcastle Road to reach the stadium.

From North

From the M62 join the M60 and continue south. Leave the M60 at junction 1, then as route for South.

By Rail

Stockport station is approx half a mile from the stadium. Arriva Trains Northern run services from Sheffield to Stockport. From London, Virgin Trains run from London Euston to directly to Stockport.

Mascot: Sharky

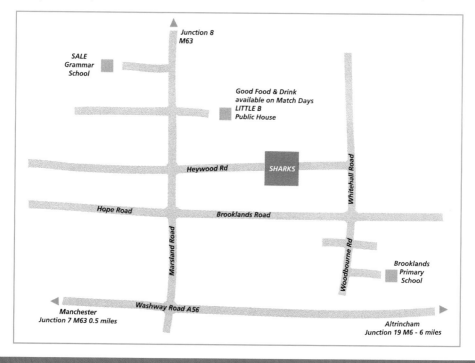

Pre-Season

Tigers' pre-season friendlies provide three away challenges against Perpignan, Cardiff Blues and Sale Sharks in the run up to the 2003/2004 season.

The warm up kicks off in earnest against Perpignan, in the heart of the south of France. On Saturday August 16, this glorious location will see an early reunion with popular former Tigers props Perry Freshwater and Franck Tournaire, the latest additions to the squad that reached this year's Heineken Cup Final. Perpignan's last matches against Leicester Tigers were in the pool groups of the 2001/2002 Heineken Cup - both were lost to Leicester, 30-31 at home, and 15-54 at Welford Road.

The second challenge for Tigers will be new Welsh regional side Cardiff Blues on August 22 (the day before the Wales vs England international at the Millennium Stadium). Tigers have played Cardiff in pre-season friendlies before - the last time being just two years ago when Tigers lost to the Welsh side 29-17. The hard fought game saw the debuts of centre Glenn Gelderbloom and lock Louis Deacon. The Welsh team has a long history in Europe, reaching the final of the Heineken Cup in the first year they qualified. The quality and proud history of their squad is reflected in the fact that Cardiff has supplied more players for Wales than any other club and a succession of Cardiff captains have led their country.

The final hurdle before the start of the season is Sharks. The match will be Sharks' first ever game at their new ground, Edgeley Park. Last season Sharks beat Tigers 29-16 in a feisty match at their old ground Heywood Road. The home match in April saw an equally thrilling battle, Tigers winning 33-20.

Sharks Chief Executive Niels de Vos said "We are delighted that the Leicester Tigers have accepted our invitation to play at our new home. Tigers have been THE team over the last five years and we look forward to an entertaining evening of rugby at our new home."

Jim Mallinder, who was equally looking forward to the game said, "Leicester Tigers are the team we wanted to play pre-season. Eighty minutes rugby against the Tigers will help prepare the players fully for the new season ahead. It is important that we have a run out on the pitch at Edgeley Park too, especially under lights."

European Preview

Stade Français

Leicester Tigers begin their Heineken Cup campaign this season with a rematch of the epic 2001 final, with Stade Français drawn in their pool group. Pool one finds Tigers also in the company of Ulster and the new Gwent Welsh regional side.

Many Tigers fans are looking forward to reliving the amazing and electrifying atmosphere that accompanied the trip to Paris, the story of the match itself would not seem out of place in a modern day fairytale. With Leon Lloyd's last minute try in the corner from a darting Healey move, converted by Tim Stimpson to win the match and the Heineken Cup 34-27. The game is considered by many Tigers players, including Neil Back and Graham Rowntree, to be the highlight of their club career to date. But what of the current Stade team, this year they enter pool one as the winners of the French Championship, having not qualified the previous year. Stade, like many of the French sides, have strengthened their squad this season with signings that include Italian international Mirco Bergamasco, former Bristol player Augustin Pichot, and Diego Dominguez, whose contract has been extended.

Stade Français' European Cup Record	
1998-99	Semi-Finals
1999-00	Quarter-Finals
2000-01	Finals
2001-02	Quarter-Finals

Ulster

Ulster are previous winners of the Heineken Cup, winning the coveted prize in 1999. Last season in the Celtic League Ulster beat Ebbw Vale away 0-19. One to watch in for his sheer game turning ability is the Irish international David Humphries, scoring the winning drop goal in last seasons Heineken Cup game against Northampton. Winners of the European Cup in 1999, they beat Colomiers 21-6 at Lansdowne Road, Dublin.

Ulster's European Cup Record	
1995-96	Cup Pool Participants
1996-97	Cup Pool Participants
1997-98	Cup Pool Participants
1998-99	Cup Winners
1999-00	Cup Pool Participants
2000-01	Cup Pool Participants
2001-02	Cup Pool Participants
2002-03	Cup Pool Participants

Gwent Dragons

This close season saw the merger of Welsh Premiership clubs under the new provincial system; Newport and Ebbw Vale are the merged sides which form the Gwent squad. The formation of the Gwent brand has not been smooth sailing, with the WRU mediating to decide the team name Gwent Dragons. The new region's games will be played at Newport's Rodney Parade, and it is believed that the playing colours, based on Newport's red away kit for last season, have been agreed upon. Despite the continued disputes off the pitch the team will be trained by the former Ebbw Vale coach Mike Ruddock, and led out by Captain and former Newport centre Andy Marinos.

Newport's European Cup Record	
2000-01	Cup Pool Participants
2001-02	Cup Pool Participants
Ebbw Vale's European Cup Record	
1998-99	Cup Pool Participants

Season Preview

After a massive shake up last year concerning the format of the Zurich Premiership, this season has no structural changes. The only difference is that it is a World Cup Year and so a number of players will be missing from the Premiership for the first half of the season.

Each club will play half its games during the World Cup where they will be missing representative players but the beauty of this period is that the playing field will be levelled and many emerging players will have the opportunity to play top quality rugby.

The Zurich Premiership kicks off on September 12, 2003. The points system remains the same as last season and is as follows:
- 4 points will be awarded for a win
- 2 points will be awarded for a draw
- 1 point will be awarded to a team that loses a match by 7 points or less
- 1 point will be awarded to a team scoring 4 tries or more in a match

Promotion/Relegation
This season there will be automatic promotion and relegation between the club that finishes bottom of the Zurich Premiership and the club who wins National Division One.

The Zurich Premiership Semi Final and Zurich Premiership Final
For the second year, the Champion Club of England will be determined at Twickenham, not at the end of the regular Zurich Premiership season. The Zurich Premiership runs for 22 rounds and finishes on Sunday 9 May. The club that tops the Zurich Premiership table will automatically qualify for the Zurich Premiership Final and the second and third clubs will play against each other for the other finalist position. The Zurich Premiership Final will be played at Twickenham on Saturday 29 May 2003 and the winning club will become the Zurich Premiership Champions.

The club who finishes at the top of the Zurich Premiership table is rewarded with an automatic place in the Zurich Premiership Final at Twickenham and will have two weekend's rest (one week if in the Heineken Cup Final). The 2nd and 3rd placed clubs in the Zurich Premiership table play each other in the Zurich Premiership Semi Final, with the 2nd placed club earning the right to home advantage. The winner will play the 1st placed club in the Zurich Premiership Final.

Zurich Wildcard 2004
Last year was the first season that clubs played off for European qualification in the Zurich Wildcard - and this format is being adopted again this season.

The top four clubs who have not automatically qualified for the Heineken Cup will enter the Zurich Wildcard where they will play a home and away leg to qualify for the Zurich Wildcard Final which is due to take place on Saturday May 29, 2004, the same day as the Zurich Premiership Final.

Powergen Cup

The Powergen Cup is England's national knockout cup and involves 128 teams in its opening stages. Leicester Tigers join the competition at round 6 which is scheduled for the weekend of November 15, 2003.

Tigers Fixtures 03-04

Date	Fixture	Opponent	Venue
Saturday 13th September 2003	Premiership	London Irish	H
Sunday 21st September	Premiership	Saracens	A
Saturday 27th September	Premiership	Newcastle Falcons	H
Saturday 4th October	Premiership	Sharks	H
Saturday 11th October	Premiership	Gloucester	A
Tuesday 14th October	Premiership	NEC Harlequins	H
Sunday 19th October	Premiership	Leeds Tykes	A
Saturday 25th October	Premiership	Northampton Saints	H
Saturday 1st November	Premiership	Bath Rugby	A
Saturday 8th November	Premiership	London Wasps	H
Saturday 15th November	Powergen Cup	Round 6	
Sunday 22nd November	Premiership	Rotherham	A
Saturday 29th November	Premiership	Bath Rugby	H
Saturday 5/6/7th December	Heineken Cup	Stade Français	A
Saturday 12/13/14th December	Heineken Cup	Gwent Dragons	H
Saturday 20th December	Premiership	Northampton Saints	A
Saturday 27th December	Premiership	Leeds Tykes	H
Wednesday 31st December	Premiership	NEC Harlequins	A
Saturday 3rd January 2004	Premiership	Gloucester	H
Saturday 9/10/11th January	Heineken Cup	Ulster	A
Saturday 16/17/18th January	Heineken Cup	Ulster	H
Saturday 23/24/25th January	Heineken Cup	Gwent Dragons	A
Saturday 30/31 Jan /1st Feb	Heineken Cup	Stade Français	H
Friday 6th February	Premiership	Sharks	A
Saturday 28th February	Powergen Cup	Quarter-Finals	
Saturday 13th March	Powergen Cup	Semi-Finals	
Sunday 4th April	Premiership	Newcastle Falcons	A
Saturday 10th April	Heineken Cup	Quarter Finals	
Saturday 17th April	Premiership	Saracens	H
Saturday 17th April	Powergen Cup	Final	
Saturday 24th April	Premiership	London Irish	A
Saturday 24th April	Heineken Cup	Semi Finals	
Saturday 1st May	Premiership	Rotherham	H
Sunday 9th May	Premiership	London Wasps	A
Saturday 15th May	Premiership	Semi-Finals	
Saturday 22nd May	Heineken Cup	Final	
Saturday 29th May	Premiership	Final	
Saturday 29th May	Wildcard	Final	

Key: ■ Home Fixtures   Away Fixtures   Powergen Fixtures   Heineken Fixtures   Other Fixtures

Join the Winning Team...

CORPORATE PARTNERS

OFFICIAL**MAIN**SPONSOR

STAND SPONSORS

TECHNOLOGY PARTNER

SHIRT SPONSOR

OFFICIAL VEHICLE SUPPLIER

JUNIOR TIGER CLUB SPONSOR

LEGAL PARTNERS

Harvey Ingram Owston
solicitors

PLAYER OF THE MONTH SPONSOR

KIT SPONSOR

TIGER CUP SPONSORS

Prima
Solutions

OFFICIAL ALE SUPPLIER

ASSOCIATE SPONSORS

OFFICIAL SPORTS DRINK SUPPLIER

The **Nautilus** Health & Fitness Group

Nautilus   SCHWINN   StairMaster   Quinto

OFFICIAL TRAVEL PARTNER

EXECUTIVE SUITE HOLDERS 2003/04

Aggregate Industries	Lafarge Aggregates
Alliance & Leicester	Masterplug
Artisan Press Ltd	Mondiboard Ltd
Barclays Bank Plc	Nexpress Group
Bostik Findley UK Ltd	NIG
Browne Jacobson	Numerica
CJC Development Company	Orange
Coach Europe Plc	PC World
David Abell	PKF
David Wilson Homes Ltd	PriceWaterhouseCoopers
Defensor Fire Detection Systems	Royal Bank of Scotland
	SCM Mircosystems
Elequip Projects Ltd	Sowden Ltd
Freethcartwright Solicitors	Spearing Waite Solicitors
Galliford Plc	The Danwood Group
Gateley Wareing	Tony Green Associates
Greshams Business Forms	Town & Country
Haas Automation	Wimpey Homes
HSBC Holdings Ltd	W R Group
Jennings Homes	

EXECUTIVE CLUB 2003/04

Adams Childrenswear	Vauxhall Motors Lt
AON Ltd	Flogas
Focus Four Ltd	Forest Gate Corby
Hewlett Packard	GSE Lining Technol
Zurich	GlaxoSmithKline
B & M Fashions	Garden Centres of
Fashion UK Ltd	Excellence

---

*To discuss partnership and sponsorship opportunities at Leicester Tigers
please call the sales office on 0116 2171 287*